Reader's Digest

# TREASURY
## OF
# BEST LOVED
# SONGS

## 114 All-Time
## Family Favorites

*Pleasure Programmed for your greater entertainment*

Editor: William L. Simon
Associates: Letitia B. Kehoe · Alan Blackman · Bruce Macomber
Supervising Editor: W. A. H. Birnie
Music arranged and edited by Dan Fox

The Reader's Digest Association, Inc.
Pleasantville, New York      Montreal

Library of Congress Catalog Card Number 71-183858
ISBN 0-89577-007-5

Printed in the United States of America

Sixth Printing, September 1981

# Index to Songs

# Index to Sections

# How to Enjoy Your New Songbook Even More

This book is truly a "by popular demand" creation, our response to the enthusiasm which greeted the first *Reader's Digest* family songbook. In this all-new collection of songs you will find selections from every decade since the turn of the century and folk songs whose echoes go back even farther. There are Broadway melodies, film hits, country music gems and inspiring songs of faith, all congenially grouped according to the exclusive *Reader's Digest* Pleasure-Programming approach to music. Moreover, on pages 4 and 5, you will find additional suggestions for song programs you and your friends are most likely to enjoy in different moods and on varying occasions.

The arrangements, prepared especially for this book, are designed for musicians of everyday ability. They are easy to play and yet they sound full, modern and thoroughly professional. Arranger Dan Fox points out the following features:

"The harmonies make restrained use of many extended chords (9ths, 11ths, etc.) as well as typical alterations used by musicians of today, and the songs have been modernized rhythmically as well. The rinky-tink syncopations in songs from the '20s and '30s have been altered to conform with today's style.

"PIANISTS will see that the harmonies are incisive and the rhythms graceful and swingy by turn. The bass lines often move in simple scale-wise fashion, arpeggios are easy to finger and the melody is right out front at all times.

"Those who have studied the so-called 'popular method' will find the melody easy to pick out (it is always stemmed up unless it stands alone) and the chord symbols unusually detailed and accurate. Although this is not always true in commercial sheet music, the popular player may assume that the root of any right-hand chord is also to be played in the bass unless otherwise specified.

"More advanced players may want to fancy things up a bit. Here are a few suggestions: The melody may sometimes be embellished with grace notes from above or below; or it can be doubled an octave lower or higher for a brighter sound; the bass line can be doubled with a lower octave for greater depth and fullness; arpeggios can be extended to cover two or more octaves; if a chord is sustained, its arpeggio may be substituted. Imaginative players will have no difficulty in thinking up more variations to suit their own style and taste.

"GUITARISTS will discover that a great deal of care has been taken to insure that their part of each arrangement is as clear and as musical as possible; the diagrams have been carefully thought out to facilitate fingering and obtain the best sound, and wherever possible, the bass note of the diagram corresponds to the bass note in the piano.

"If you have a guitar-playing friend, one of you can play the melody in single notes and the other the chords. If you have another friend who plays bass guitar, let him play from the lower staff, and you have a group. In any case, there is something here for the guitarist of every ability, from blues and folk songs using only a few chords to modern ballads and jazz songs which use 9ths, 13ths, passing harmonies and altered chords.

"ORGAN PLAYERS, too, will find these arrangements interesting, challenging and fun to play. The small notes under the lower staff indicate the proper bass note. The range of the bass line has been kept within an octave in order that it can be played on any model electronic or pipe organ. Like pianists, players who have studied the popular method will find the melody easy to pick out. Pedals are indicated by the small notes below the staff, and the left hand can fill in chords as indicated by the symbols.

"SINGERS will appreciate the clarity with which these songs are presented. There are no confusing repeat signs, and page turns occur only where a song runs for three or more pages. The words are printed in a type face which is easily legible even when reading over someone's shoulder.

"Finally, players of the VIOLIN, FLUTE, MELODICA, HARMONICA and other C-melody instruments can play the melody from the top line of each system, or use the melody notes as a guide and create improvisations based on the chord symbols above the top staff."

For every singer, instrumentalist, soloist or family group, there are many hours of exciting musical fun and exhilaration awaiting you in these pages. We hope you will enjoy them to the fullest.

THE EDITORS

# Pleasure Programs

## Songs Introduced in Films

*\*Academy Award Winner*

## Songs Introduced in Broadway Shows

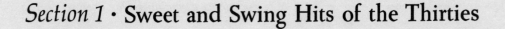

# Star Dust

*F*ittingly, your TREASURY OF BEST LOVED SONGS opens with what many believe is the best loved song of the 20th century. When the editors started compiling the repertoire, "Star Dust" was the first song that came to mind, and in this special instance they decided to include the introductory verse to the song–a portion that is every bit as lovely as the chorus, and almost as familiar.

How can you actually spell out the magic of "Star Dust"? One of America's greatest lyricists, the late Oscar Hammerstein II, tried in the preface of his book Lyrics: "'Star Dust' rambles and roams like a truant schoolboy in a meadow. Its structure is loose, its pattern complex. Yet it has attained the kind of long-lived popularity that few songs can claim. What has it got? I'm not certain. I know only that it is beautiful and I like to hear it. It is a mood-creating song. It has repose and wistfulness. It is something very special, all by itself. Anyone who tried to imitate it would be a fool."

"Star Dust" has become "our song" to millions of couples–the unrivaled "favorite song" of our century. Yet, oddly, "Star Dust" was never really a "hit" in the accepted Tin Pan Alley sense. Although the song was published in 1929, its first million-selling record wasn't made until 1940–an instrumental by Artie Shaw and his orchestra. But today "Star Dust" has been recorded in countless different versions; it has been arranged and printed for every range of voice, every solo instrument, and just about every imaginable combination of voices and instruments. It probably is the only song which ever had recordings made of its verse alone, without the familiar chorus.

The "Star Dust" saga began one fall night in 1927. Hoagy Carmichael, recently graduated attorney, pianist and avid jazz fan, had returned to Indiana University, hoping perhaps to piece together some fragmented memories of his undergraduate days. Inevitably he visited a romantic spot then called the "spooning wall." Sitting there alone he looked up at the clear, star-filled sky and a phrase of music formed in his mind. He rushed over to the Book Nook, a campus restaurant, to work it out on the piano. Later he played the tune for his old roommate, Stuart Gorrell, who gave "Star Dust" its name.

It seems odd to us today that the most sentimental of ballads was conceived by Hoagy as a swingy–almost ragtime–piano piece. It wasn't until 1929 that Victor Young, then an arranger for the Isham Jones Orchestra, was inspired to slow it down, changing it from a "piano piece" to a "song." Mitchell Parish was asked in to write the lyrics and "Star Dust" was on its way. Parish recalls that Walter Winchell played a big part in bringing it to the public's ear. "He was so crazy about it that he plugged it almost daily in his column. Even years later, I remember sitting in the Copa with him one night listening to Nat "King" Cole. Nat sang "Star Dust" to a beautiful arrangement by Gordon Jenkins and everybody in the place, including Winchell, had a tear in his eye. I've heard the song done thousands of times, but I remember Nat's rendition above all others."

Words by: Mitchell Parish          Music by: Hoagy Carmichael

8

# Moonglow

Hudson and De Lange wanted to be bandleaders, but both proved more successful—individually and as a team—writing songs. In the early '30s, Hudson was asked to put together a band for an extended engagement at the Graystone Ballroom in Detroit. He found himself with a full "book" of arrangements but nothing suitable for a theme song. He solved the problem in just ten minutes by writing "Moonglow." Two years later De Lange added the lyrics, and the song was an instant hit. This led to the formation of the short-lived Hudson–De Lange Orchestra.

**By: Will Hudson, Eddie De Lange and Irving Mills**

# Blue Moon

"Blue Moon"—as we know it—was the only Rodgers and Hart hit that wasn't written specially for a screen or stage production. The first version, entitled "Prayer," was composed in 1933 for Jean Harlow to sing in a film called Hollywood Revue. The project was scrapped. In 1934, Hart wrote new lyrics and it became "The Bad in Every Man," sung by Shirley Ross in the William Powell film Manhattan Melodrama—and quickly forgotten. A third set of lyrics, suggested by the publisher that same year, produced "Blue Moon." In 1948, Billy Eckstine "revived" it with a million-selling recording; in 1961, a rock group, called the Marcels, doubled that sale with a version in which Rodgers' melody was altered beyond recognition and Hart's words were unintelligible.

**Music by: Richard Rodgers**

**Words by: Lorenz Hart**

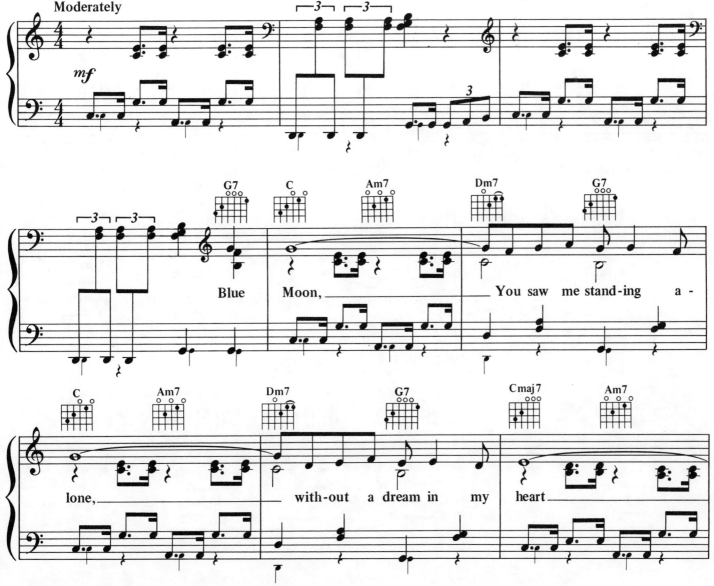

# I'm in the Mood for Love

*Composer McHugh loved to tell this story of his boyhood music lessons with his mother: Mrs. McHugh encouraged him to improvise melodies on the piano. If one sounded original, she gave him a nickel; if it did not, he received a smart rap on the knuckles. This "original," composed for the 1935 film Every Night at Eight, earned a considerable number of nickels for McHugh.*

**Words and Music by:**

**Jimmy McHugh and Dorothy Fields**

# I'm Gonna Sit Right Down and Write Myself a Letter

When Ahlert first played this song for his family, Fred, Jr., a successful music publisher today, recalls, "I was eight at the time. I said it was awful, but Dad assured me it would be a big hit. Then it lay on the publisher's shelf for a year until somebody showed it to Fats Waller. He loved it at first sight!" His recording made Ahlert Sr.'s prophecy come true.

**Words by: Joe Young**

**Music by: Fred E. Ahlert**

19

# Red Sails in the Sunset

Words by: Jimmy Kennedy
Music by: Hugh Williams

*Lyricist Kennedy and his artist-sister were standing on a cliff in their native Donegal, Ireland, in 1935 watching the spreading sunset frame the red sail of a local boat. "You should paint that," he said. "I will, if you'll write a song about it," she answered. Both kept the bargain. Will Grosz, using the pen name Hugh Williams, set Kennedy's lyrics to music.*

Moderately slow

*p dreamily*

*mp* Red Sails In The Sun - set, 'Way out on the sea,

Oh! car - ry my loved one Home safe - ly to me.

He sailed at the dawn - ing, All day I've been blue,

# MOON OVER MIAMI

*After several years of pressure and frustration in Hollywood during the '30s, composer Burke bought a one-way ticket back to New York, where, with lyricist Leslie, he produced six Number One hits in three*

*years. When Burke played this melody for Leslie, the latter felt the theme called for "Moon over something." They finally settled on Miami, deciding to cash in on the current Florida building boom.*

**Words by: Edgar Leslie**

**Music by: Joe Burke**

Moderately slow, but with a swing

Moon O - ver Mi - a - mi, Shine on my love and

me,___ So we can stroll___ be - side the roll, Of the

roll - ing sea. Moon O - ver Mi -

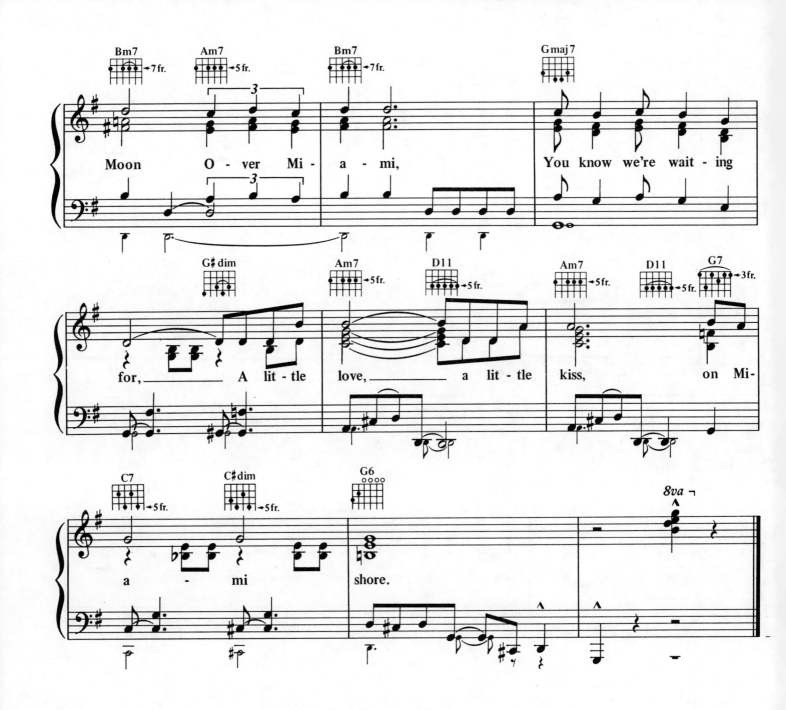

# On the Sunny Side of the Street

For some reason, male songwriters far outnumber the women. But few men have matched the success of lyricist Dorothy Fields, of the show-business Fields family. (Her father was Lew Fields, the "Dutch" comedian of Weber and Fields fame; her brother was Herbert Fields, author of Broadway musicals.) She first collaborated with Jimmy McHugh in the hit-studded Blackbirds of 1928. The following year the same team produced this song, as well as "Exactly Like You," for Lew Leslie's International Revue. "On the Sunny Side of the Street" was introduced in the show by Harry Richman.

Words by: Dorothy Fields
Music by: Jimmy McHugh

# In the Chapel in the Moonlight

The chapel silhouetted in moonlight in this peaceful, pastoral song was a 100-year-old church located at Broadway and 55th Street—right in the bustling heart of New York City! Today the site of the church is a parking lot, but the song remains very much with us, a hit with each of the succeeding generations.

By: Billy Hill

# Penthouse Serenade
## (When We're Alone)

*During the depression some unemployed actors produced a co-op show called* The Nine O'Clock Revue. *The songwriters were given 24 hours to complete the score, and this song, which was staged satirically, was hardly expected to be a hit. But Paul Whiteman selected "Penthouse Serenade" for a special New Year's Day broadcast on which his orchestra, performing in Chicago, accompanied film star Bebe Daniels, who sang the song in Los Angeles. It skyrocketed from there.*

**By: Will Jason and Val Burton**

© 1931 Famous Music Corp. Copyright renewed

31

# DEEP PURPLE

*De Rose composed "Deep Purple" in 1934 as a piano composition, inspired no doubt by George Gershwin's "Rhapsody in Blue." Parish's lyrics were not added until 1939, and Larry*

*Clinton's recording made a star of his vocalist Bea Wain. The song became such a favorite of baseball's Babe Ruth that on each of his birthdays De Rose personally played and sang it for him.*

**Words by: Mitchell Parish**

**Music by: Peter De Rose**

When the Deep Pur-ple falls o-ver sleep-y gar-den walls, and the stars be-gin to flick-er in the sky, Thru the mist of a mem-o-ry you wan-der back to me, breath-ing my name with a sigh.

# It Looks Like Rain in Cherry Blossom Lane

*Together Burke and Leslie wrote many Number One songs, but this one yielded the biggest return in terms of working time expended. Once they had the catchy title, it took them just 20 minutes to complete the song.*

**Words by: Edgar Leslie**

**Music by: Joe Burke**

Moderately, with a lilt

It Looks Like Rain In Cher-ry Blos-som Lane, The sun-shine of your smile's no long-er there._____ It Looks Like Rain In Cher-ry Blos-som Lane, Your

34

# Blue Hawaii

### Words and Music by:
### Leo Robin and Ralph Rainger

*When Robin and Rainger had completed their score for the Bing Crosby film Waikiki Wedding, lyricist Robin felt it lacked a real potential hit. "Ralph," he told his partner, "when you get up tomorrow, go to the piano and jot down the first tune that pops into your head." He did, and that tune was "Blue Hawaii."*

*Guitar players may do a long slide to this chord using a knife handle to hold the strings down.

# HEART AND SOUL

During a brief period in the Swing Era, the Hollywood film studios produced a series of "short subjects" featuring dance bands, usually playing their established hits. But only one "short," A Song Is Born (1938) effectively introduced a hit. The band was Larry Clinton's, with vocalist Bea Wain, and the song was "Heart and Soul," Carmichael and Loesser's first collaboration. Carmichael was an established composer at the time, but Loesser—later a creator of both

words and music—was still only a lyricist. Carmichael told the Digest that the song kicked around the backrooms of Paramount Pictures for a month before it was assigned to any picture. During that period "the best use the song got was for Anthony Quinn's voice practice." This was before Quinn became a star. The writers were disappointed when their song was launched in a minor production, but the disappointment was short-lived as Clinton's recording became a big seller.

**Words by: Frank Loesser**

**Music by: Hoagy Carmichael**

38

40

# The Glory of Love

*Hill, a one-time cowpoke, classical violin student and miner, was working in New York as a doorman. But depression-time tips were meager and he turned to song-writing to supplement his income. He struck gold with "The Last Round-Up" and "Wagon Wheels," then with "The Glory of Love" in 1936. In 1967 a new generation discovered this song in the film* Guess Who's Coming to Dinner.

By:
Billy Hill

win a lit-tle, lose a lit-tle, And al-ways have the

blues a lit-tle: That's the sto-ry of That's The Glo-ry Of

(No chords till end)

Love.

*pp*

In 1931 Rudy Vallee made some changes in the lyrics of this English song and introduced it on his Thursday night radio program. By the following Saturday, 10,000 copies of the music were

# Good Night Sweetheart

sold. Vallee planned to record the song, but the Victor company gave the recording assignment to Wayne King. Vallee became so infuriated that he broke his contract.

By: Ray Noble, Jimmy Campbell and Reg Connelly

American Version by: Rudy Vallee

# SMOKE GETS IN YOUR EYES

It was 1933, the depths of the depression, and shows were closing up and down Broadway. But *Roberta* played on, thanks to this plaintive song, first intended by Kern as an instrumental interlude to fill in during scene changes. He dusted off a march he

had composed some time earlier as a theme for an unproduced radio series, slowed down the tempo and then decided it could use lyrics after all. On opening night, Tamara and the song brought down the house. Later, Irene Dunne sang it in the film version.

**Words by:**

Otto Harbach

**Music by:**

Jerome Kern

46

# Can't Help Lovin' Dat Man

Today it is hard for us to conceive that this, one of the most typical and famous examples of the "torch song" idiom, was written to be performed at a fast tempo—specifically to set up a dance sequence in Show Boat. In that show it was sung by both Helen Morgan, as the tragic mulatto Julie, and by Norma Terris, as the ingenue Magnolia. But it was Miss Morgan, with her big dewy eyes and tremulous delivery, who put her personal seal on the song, singing it in nightclubs—perched on top of the piano—at a much slower tempo.

Words by: Oscar Hammerstein II                    Music by: Jerome Kern

50

back dat day is fine,____ The sun will shine.

He can come home____ as late as can be,____ Home with-out him____ ain't

no home to me____ Can't Help Lov-in' Dat Man____ of

mine.

# Make Believe

When Alexander Woollcott introduced composer Kern to Edna Ferber, author of
the best-selling book Show Boat, Kern remarked, "I got a copy of your book and
tried to read it, but I had to keep putting it down." The lady was visibly shocked
until he continued, "I had to keep putting it down to go to the piano to work out
the melodies that kept popping into my head." "Make Believe" was one of those
melodies heard in Kern's memorable musical version of Miss Ferber's novel.

**Words by:**
Oscar Hammerstein II

**Music by:**
Jerome Kern

# Why Do I Love You?

Knowing that composer Kern despised the word "Cupid" in lyrics, Hammerstein contrived a set for this song that started with "Cupid knows the way" and continued with a string of clichés about the god of love. Kern enjoyed the joke—especially when he saw the real lyrics. He had the "Cupid" version framed, and it hung in his study for many years.

**Words by: Oscar Hammerstein II**

**Music by: Jerome Kern**

# Look for the Silver Lining

Words by:
Buddy DeSylva

*Ziegfeld asked Kern and author P.G. Wodehouse to write a show for his superstar Marilyn Miller, but Wodehouse was busy finishing a serial for the Saturday Evening Post. He reminded Kern about several songs left "in the trunk" from earlier flops. One that Kern dusted off was "Look for the Silver Lining." It became the biggest hit in the smashingly successful Sally.*

Music by:
Jerome Kern

# All the Things You Are

Nobody expected this song to become a hit, let alone an immortal favorite. Kern admittedly composed the complex melody for his own satisfaction, but he was certain the public would never hum it. Then the show in which it appeared, Very Warm for May (1939), was a disaster. Yet "All the Things You Are" has survived, a monument to the public's good taste.

Words by: Oscar Hammerstein II
Music by: Jerome Kern

58

59

# Hello, Dolly!

*The song "Hello, Dolly!" was strong enough to help keep the musical of the same name alive for the second longest Broadway run in history. (Fiddler on the Roof passed it in July of 1971.) It holds the record for the largest sum ever paid in a copyright infringement settlement, thanks to the similarity of its opening phrases to a part of the song "Sunflower," a short-lived hit of 1948.*

**Words and Music by: Jerry Herman**

60

# Mame

**Words and Music by:
Jerry Herman**

*After the success of the title song of Hello, Dolly!, it was only natural for the producers of Herman's next show, Mame, to request a similarly catchy self-advertising "theme." Herman resisted, insisting that "lightning never strikes twice," but finally he broke down, dashed off this song in a few minutes and decided he liked it even better than "Dolly." Mame made Angela Lansbury the brightest light on the Broadway musical stage.*

Moderate Dixieland tempo

You coax the blues right out__ of the horn,

Mame.__ You charm the husk right off__ of the

64

# I'll Never Fall in Love Again

*According to Bacharach, "This was written the day after I got out of the hospital in Boston. I was there one week with pneumonia while our show* Promises, Promises *was trying out. Perhaps that was Hal's inspiration for the lines: 'What do you get when you kiss a guy?' etc. It was the fastest song we wrote for the show (one day), the most successful and perhaps the most hazy, for I had no idea what I was doing that first day out of the hospital."*

**Words by: Hal David**        **Music by: Burt Bacharach**

# This Guy's in Love with You

*After an extraordinary string of successes with his Tijuana Brass on his own A & M record label, Herb Alpert decided it was time to try something new—singing. For his TV special in April 1968 he turned to top writers Bacharach and David for a new song tailored to the special quality of his voice. They came up with this tune. It went over so well that Alpert recorded it, and "This Guy's in Love with You" became one of his biggest hits.*

**Words by: Hal David**          **Music by: Burt Bacharach**

68

When you smile,_ I can tell we know each oth-er ver-y well. How

can I show you I'm glad I got to know you, 'cause

I've heard_ some talk. They say you think I'm fine.

This guy's in love, and what I'd do to make you mine.

Tell me now,_ is it so? Don't let me be the last to know. My

# What the World Needs Now Is Love

*In form it's a syncopated jazz waltz—a rarity in pop music, even for the unconventional Bacharach and David. But its message is that of a spiritual and, in fact, its joy-through-affirmation jubilation has made the song an inspiring addition to latter-day church services. David recalls the struggle he had with the lyrics—with his list of objects of which "we don't need another." But once he had hit upon the word "mountain," he had found his key. He discarded all man-made things from the list and stuck with God's creations.*

**Words by: Hal David**     **Music by: Burt Bacharach**

love, It's the on - ly thing\_\_\_\_ that there's just\_\_\_\_\_ too

lit - tle of. What The World Needs Now Is Love, sweet

love, No, not just for some,\_\_ but for ev - 'ry - one.\_\_\_\_

\_\_\_ No, not just for some,\_\_ oh, but just for

ev - 'ry - - one.\_\_\_\_

# (They Long to Be)
# Close to You

### Words by: Hal David
### Music by: Burt Bacharach

Here we have one of the most melodic, charming and enduring songs by the prolific Bacharach-David team, but one of the few that did not become an instant hit. They wrote it in 1963 but were unable to interest anyone in recording it until the Carpenters came along in 1970. This soft-harmonizing brother-sister team had its own five-year history of rejection, trying to buck the hard-rock tide. Then suddenly the combination of their warm sound and this warm tune seems to have captivated all the generations.

75

# DOWNTOWN

**Words and Music by: Tony Hatch**

In 1961 English singer Petula Clark married a Frenchman and moved to Paris, finding there a success that had eluded her for years back home. In fact, she was about to give up recording in English altogether. Then recording producer Hatch brought three songs to France, hoping to lure her back to his studio. When she was unmoved by them, in desperation he played a new melody he had just composed, called "Downtown," inspired by a trip to New York. "Write a lyric and I'll do it," said Pet. Her recording sold more than 3 million copies.

When you're a-lone___ and life is mak-ing you lone-ly, you can al-ways go___ Down-town. When you've got wor-ries, all the noise and the hur-ry seems to help I know.___ Down-town. Just lis-ten to the mu-sic of the traf-fic in the ci-ty. Ling-er on the side-walk where the

# Let It Be Me

When an American publisher obtains the rights to a foreign song, he customarily enlists several writers to do English lyrics, then selects the set he considers best. In this case, Curtis didn't wait for an assignment —he had heard composer Bécaud's own French recording of the song "Je t'appartiens" and felt it could be as big here as Bécaud's other hits —"What Now My Love?" and "It Must Be Him." When the French star came to New York to appear at the Plaza Hotel's Persian Room, Curtis showed up with his "Let It Be Me" lyrics and won instant approval. Then a Mexican-American singer, Florencia Bisenta de Casillas Martinez Cardona (better known as Vikki Carr), who had created the hit recording of "It Must Be Him," made "Let It Be Me" her second Bécaud smash in a row.

**English Words by: Mann Curtis**     **French Words by: Pierre Delanoe**

**Music by: Gilbert Bécaud**

*Melody may be doubled 8ᵛᵉ higher until the sign ⊕.

# The Girl from Ipanema

*A new music was proliferating in Brazil. It was the bossa nova, a fresh blend of the samba with "cool" modern jazz, topped with lovely, languid melodies by writers such as Antonio Carlos Jobim and Luiz Bonfa. American jazzmen like Stan Getz and Charlie Byrd picked up the music and began building an enthusiastic audience. But when music businessmen ignored the trend, Jobim himself came to New York to stir things up a bit. One convert to his music was the lyricist Norman Gimbel, who wrote this English lyric to "Ipanema" based roughly on Vinicius de Moraes' Portuguese original. Getz's 1963 recording of the song, with Jobim at the piano, won the "Record of the Year" Grammy award of the National Academy of Recording Arts and Sciences.*

**English words by: Norman Gimbel**　　　　**Original words by: Vinicius de Moraes**

**Music by: Antonio Carlos Jobim**

Tall and tan and young and love-ly The Girl From I-pa-ne-ma goes walk-ing, and when she pass-es, each one she pass-es goes "Aah!"

day when she walks to the sea ___ she looks straight a - head not at me.

Tall and tan and young and love - ly The Girl From I - pa - ne - ma goes walk - ing, and

when she pass - es I smile, but she does - n't see. She just does - n't

see. No, she does - n't see. ___

# Strangers in the Night

Kaempfert, an orchestra leader, songwriter and arranger from Hamburg, Germany, was already well
established with the American public when he wrote
this, his biggest hit. His own band's recordings of
"Wonderland by Night" and "Red Roses for a Blue
Lady" had been million-sellers, and other artists
scanned each Kaempfert record release, watching for
new song material. It was not Kaempfert, however, but
Frank Sinatra who made "Strangers in the Night" the
biggest success of 1965. When the star added his
"Scoobie Doobie Doo" to the tail of his otherwise romantic performance, many listeners cringed, but—no
doubt—it made the record unforgettable and the biggest seller of Frank's long and fabulous career.

Words by:
Charles Singleton & Eddie Snyder
Music by: Bert Kaempfert

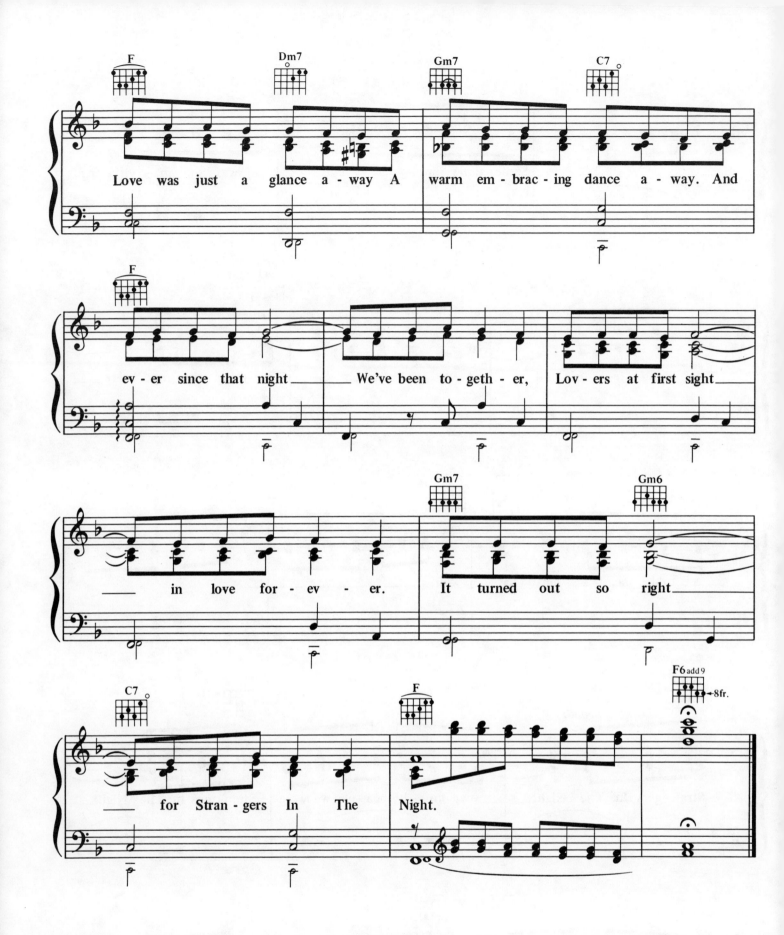

Love was just a glance a-way A warm em-brac-ing dance a-way. And

ev-er since that night ___ We've been to-geth-er, Lov-ers at first sight ___

___ in love for-ev-er. It turned out so right ___

___ for Stran-gers In The Night.

# Goin' Out of My Head

*This song, written in 1963 by rock 'n' roll star Teddy Randazzo for Little Anthony and the Imperials, was an immediate hit with the younger set, but it didn't reach the adult public* *until 1968, when the Lettermen made their recording of it. Their version struck a happy balance between melodic tradition and rock, establishing the song as a classic.*

**Words and Music by: Teddy Randazzo and Bobby Weinstein**

can't think of an-y-thing but you._____ And I

think I'm go-ing out of my head 'Cause I can't ex-plain the tears that I

shed o - ver you,_____ o - ver you._____

_____ I see you each morn-ing but you just walk past me you

don't e - ven know that I ex - ist._____ Go - in' Out Of My

# New World in the Morning

Singer and composer Roger Whittaker, a native of Nairobi, Kenya, brought this neo-spiritual to the world's largest song festival, in Rio de Janeiro, in 1969, and walked off with three gold medals. Both as a writer and performer he suddenly found himself an international star.

**Words and Music by: Roger Whittaker**

# Love Is Blue

In 1968, "Love Is Blue" was the most popular song in the world.
Everywhere, that is, except in the country of its origin—France!
True, hard rock was the rage everywhere when the song was en-
tered in the Eurovision song competition, and the judges awarded
it a spot near the bottom of the list. But an American publisher
heard Paul Mauriat's recording and fell in love with it. He arranged for its release here and went to work on it. The result—
the largest sheet-music sale in many years and recordings by some
350 artists. But the song has never become popular in France.

**Words by: Bryan Blackburn**
**Music by: André Popp**
**French Words by: Pierre Cour**

93

94

# Quiet Nights of Quiet Stars
## (Corcovado)

*In Rio de Janeiro in 1962, lyricist Lees persuaded composer Jobim to let him translate some of his Portuguese lyrics into English. With this song Lees hoped that he was successful in retaining the mood, thoughts and rhyming characteristics, "including the sudden and unexpected break of rhyme in the last lines, which fits the unresolved nature of the melody." One reading of this little masterpiece shows just how successful he was.*

**Original Words and Music by:**
**Antonio Carlos Jobim**
**English Words by: Gene Lees**

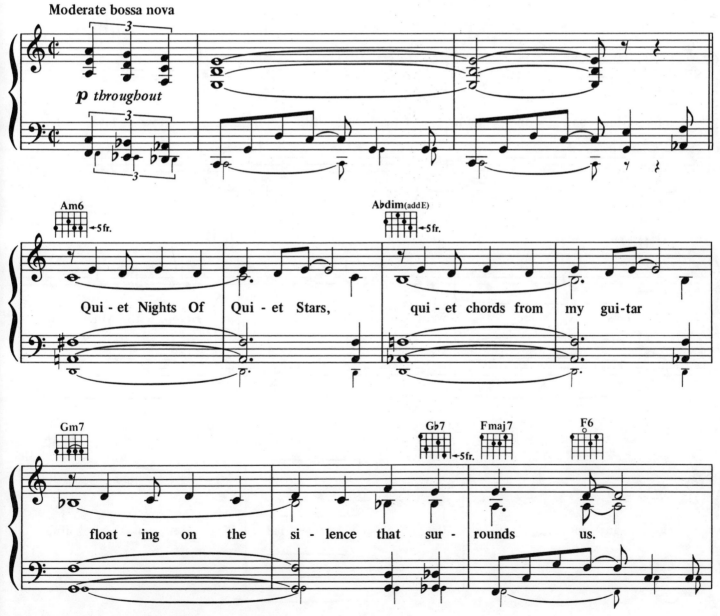

# Red Roses
# for a Blue Lady

The collaboration of songwriters Tepper and Brodsky began when both were 11 years old and lasted for 38 years—probably a record in the fickle world of pop music. When they composed "Red Roses" in 1948, Guy Lombardo and Vaughn Monroe made it a "respectable" hit, but in 1965 German bandleader Bert Kaempfert discovered the song, and his version, along with two others, made the Top 10 that year.

**Words and Music by:
Sid Tepper and Roy Brodsky**

flow-ers chase her blues a-way. Wrap up some

Red Ros-es For A Blue La-dy,

Send them to the sweet-est gal in town. And

if they do the trick, I'll hur-ry back to pick Your

best white or-chid for her wed-ding gown.

# I Wish You Love

**English Words by: Albert A. Beach**

**French Words by: Charles Trenet**

**Music by: Charles Trenet**

*When writing the English lyrics for this French song, Beach could hear the couple next door engaged in a verbal free-for-all. Hate words bounced through the thin walls, and writing a love lyric seemed impossible. He started to reread Through the Looking-Glass and got no farther than Alice's remark to her kitten: "First there's the room you can see through the glass—that's just the same as our drawing room, only things go the other way." Beach started "mirroring" the neighbors' hate words into opposites. His lyric was at the publisher's the next day.*

I wish you blue-birds in the spring to give your heart a song to sing and then a kiss but more than this I Wish You Love.

And in Ju-ly a lem-on-ade to cool you in some leaf-y glade I wish you health and more than wealth I Wish You

# I Want to Hold Your Hand

The Beatles, those four interesting, talented lads from Liverpool, began setting the music world on its ear in 1962, and the changing character and content of their songs blazed new paths in every field of music—pop, country, folk, even symphonic. This early Beatles hit, for example, gave Arthur Fiedler and the Boston Pops Orchestra their biggest hit since "Jalousie."

**Words and Music by:**

**John Lennon and Paul McCartney**

Oh yeh, I'll_____ tell you some-thing I think you'll un-der-stand. Then I'll_____ say that some-thing, I Want To Hold Your_ Hand. I Want To Hold Your Hand._____ I Want To Hold Your Hand. Oh_ please_ say to me

# Scarlet Ribbons
## (for Her Hair)

*The "miracle" that happens to the little girl in "Scarlet Ribbons" is hardly more eerie than the circumstances under which Segal wrote the lyrics. A guest at the home of Evelyn Danzig one evening, he listened to her play a haunting little étude that stayed in his ear. That very night he started to write. The melody had cast a spell over him and he lost intellectual control over the task he had set himself. In a state of emotional excitement bordering on religious experience, Segal discovered that the song virtually wrote itself.*

**Words by: Jack Segal**             **Music by: Evelyn Danzig**

*Watch the dynamics; they are very important.

scar - let rib - bons for her hair. *cresc.*

If I live to be two hun - dred, I will nev - er

*slower* // *in tempo* know from where,___ Came those love - ly scar - let rib - bons,

scar - let rib - bons for___ her___ hair. *dying away*

# Matilda, Matilda!

*"Matilda," a West Indian calypso, is identified almost exclusively with singer Harry Belafonte. If Harry may be said to have a theme song, this is it. He recorded it first in 1953, and then several times later. His live performances of the number sometimes run as long as 15 minutes as he winds up a concert exercising all his considerable charm and humor to make his audience sing the chorus. "And now—all the big spenders!" or "All ladies over 40!" The latter usually draws a complete silence, followed by a gust of laughter and another—this time successful—appeal to the ladies to sing.*

**Words and Music by: Norman Span**

Ma - til - da___ Ma - til - da She take me mon - ey and run Ve - ne - zue - lah.

(No chords)
*last time, end here* VERSE

Five hun - dred dol - lars friends___ I lost what made me sell me cat___ and horse Hey - a

*Repeat chorus*

Ma - til - da She take me mon - ey and run Ve - ne - zue - lah. Ev - 'ry - bod - y!

*Verse 2.* (Well, de money was) just inside me bed,
   Stuck up in de pillow beneath me head. Don't you know
   CHORUS

*Verse 3.* (Well, me friends) nevah to love again,
   All de money gone in vain, Hey-a
   CHORUS

109

# Michael, Row the Boat Ashore

*Modern folklore collectors tell us that "Michael" originated in the islands off the coast of Georgia, where it has been sung since slave days. It is fairly unusual in that it is both a spiritual and a work song–specifically, a sea chantey–which was sung by slaves rowing plantation riverboats. When the load was heavy, they invoked the help of the Archangel Michael, intoning the lines to the stroke of the oars. In 1961, the Highwaymen, a vocal quintet, made the song a universal favorite with their million-selling record.*

**Very steady and not too fast**

Mi - chael row the boat a - shore hal - le - lu -

iah, Mi - chael row the boat a - shore hal - le -

*Repeat for additional verses*

2. *Jordan's river is chilly and cold, halleluiah,*
   *Jordan's river is chilly and cold, halleluiah,*
   *Jordan's river is wide and deep, halleluiah,*
   *Jordan's river is wide and deep, halleluiah,*
   *Michael, row the boat ashore, oh, yes.*

3. *Gabriel, blow the trumpet horn, halleluiah,*
   *Gabriel, blow the trumpet horn, halleluiah.*
   *Michael's boat is a gospel boat, halleluiah,*
   *Michael's boat is a gospel boat, halleluiah,*
   *Michael, row the boat ashore, oh, yes.*

# The Fox

*Youngsters will probably love this fox eternally because the canny little fellow defied adult authority and got away with it. Although thought to have been a nursery favorite even in the eighteenth century, the song first appeared in print in Scotland in 1832 in a small collection edited, it is believed, by the Scottish publisher James Ballantyne. More than a hundred years later American folk singers such as Burl Ives, Pete Seeger and Woody Guthrie rediscovered "The Fox" with its bright, singable lyrics and have made it a highlight of every children's concert.*

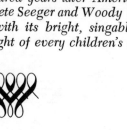

**Traditional**

Moderate Calypso tempo

The Fox went out___ on a chil-ly night___ Prayed for the moon to give him light___ For he'd man-y a mile___ to go that night___ Be-

fore he reached the town - o, town - o town - o He'd man - y a mile to go that night Be-

Repeat for additional verses

fore he reached the town - o.

2. He ran till he found a big, big pen
Where the ducks and the geese were put therein,
"Tonight two of you will grease my chin
Before I leave this town - o, town - o, town - o,
Tonight two of you will grease my chin
Before I leave this town - o."

3. He grabbed a big goose by the neck,
And threw a duck across his back;
He didn't mind their quack, quack, quack
And their four legs dangling down - o, down - o, down - o,
He didn't mind their quack, quack, quack
And their four legs dangling down -o.

4. He ran till he got back to his den;
Where little ones waited, eight, nine, ten.
"Daddy," they said, "better go back again,
For it must be a very fine town - o, town - o, town - o,"
"Daddy," they said, "better go back again,
For it must be a very fine town - o"

5. Then the fox and his wife without any strife
Cut up the birds with a fork and knife;
For the best supper they'd had in their life,
And the little ones chewed on the bones - o, bones - o, bones - o,
For the best supper they'd had in their life,
And the little ones chewed on the bones - o.

# MIDNIGHT SPECIAL

*This rocking folk song probably originated on a Texas prison farm. The train that inspired it may have been the Golden Gate Limited, which pulled out of Houston at midnight headed for San Francisco. Less than an hour later its "ever-lovin'" headlight shone through the prison bars, stirring fantasies of freedom. The great folksinger, Huddie Ledbetter, better known as Leadbelly, knew that particular prison all too well. In his youth he was a rambler and a "rounder." He knew the rural South, from its churches to its chain gangs. He remembered hundreds of songs heard from anonymous singers—which he reshaped with his powerful voice and his hard-driving 12-string guitar. "Midnight Special" was just one of the many songs he brought to light.*

**Traditional**

2. A knife and a fork on the table,
   And nothin' in your pan;
   But just say a word about it,
   And you're in trouble with that man.
   Chorus

3. Yonder Miss Rosie's a-comin'.
   You're askin' me how do I know?
   I know her by her apron,
   And by the dress she wore.
   Chorus

4. She's bringin' me some coffee,
   She's bringin' me some tea.
   Man, she's bringin' just about ev'rything
   But not the jailhouse key!
   Chorus

# God Bless' the Child

In her autobiography, Lady Sings the Blues, *Billie Holiday tells about growing up on the streets of Harlem, where she learned firsthand about prostitution, drugs and the blues. She also learned the special meaning of the proverb "God blesses the child that's got his own," a black variation on "God helps him who helps himself." In 1941, when she was on the brink of stardom, she and Arthur Herzog Jr. made this the basis of a song—one which was rendered especially poignant by Billie's own singing. Billie died in 1959, but in the late '60s Aretha Franklin revived her song, followed by other black stylists and numerous young folk singers. In 1969 it reached its biggest audience when it was included in an LP by* Blood, Sweat and Tears *that sold more than 3 million copies.*

**Words and Music by: Arthur Herzog Jr. and Billie Holiday**

# Section 5 · The Tuneful Twenties

# Side by Side

**By: Harry Woods**

Songwriting was just a sideline to Harry Woods, who preferred to spend his time among fishermen, sailors and farmers. Still he managed to toss off dozens of great songs including "When the Red, Red Robin Comes Bob, Bob, Bobbin' Along," "I'm Looking Over a Four-Leaf Clover," "Try a Little Tenderness" and the theme songs for Kate Smith and Rudy Vallee. Woods was born without fingers on his left hand, but he learned to perform prodigious feats at the piano with his large, powerful right, while his left, playing almost entirely on the black keys, managed to thump out a terrific bass. Introduced in 1927, "Side by Side" —with its very appealing note of sunny optimism and togetherness —came into its own during the Great Depression.

Oh we ain't got a barrel of money. Maybe we're ragged and funny but we'll travel along singin' a song

Moderate ragtime feeling

© 1927, renewed, Shapiro, Bernstein & Co., Inc.

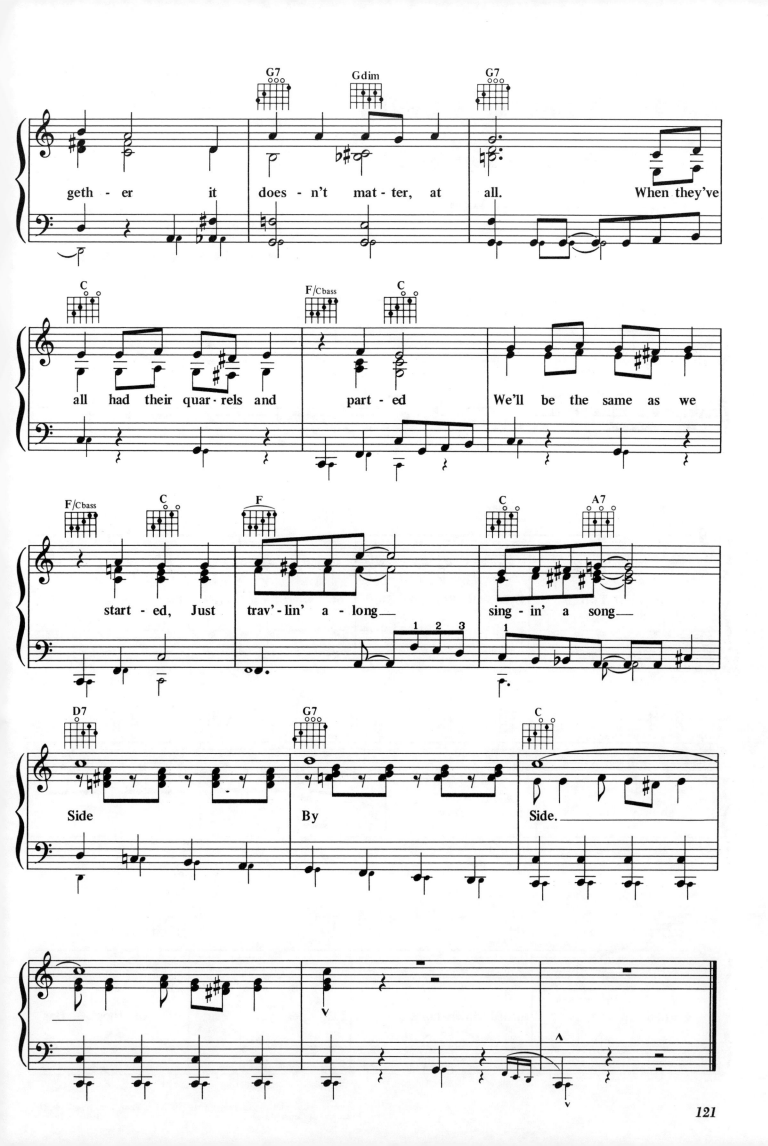

# Five Foot Two, Eyes of Blue

## (Has Anybody Seen My Girl?)

*Few songs of the Charleston Era have captured its wacky, high-spirited, devil-may-care flavor as perfectly as this delightful ditty. And few songs have been so easy to remember and so inviting to "sing-along" addicts. Composer Henderson wrote it in 1925, the year before he teamed with Buddy DeSylva and Lew Brown to form the quintessential songwriting team of the decade. That was the year that he also wrote "I'm Sitting on Top of the World" and "Alabamy Bound."*

**Words by: Sam Lewis and Joe Young**
**Music by: Ray Henderson**

Five Foot Two,_ Eyes Of Blue,_ But oh! what those_ five foot could do,_ Has an-y-bod-y seen my girl?

Turned up nose_ turned down hose,_ Flap-per, yes_ sir, one of those._ Has

# I Can't Give You Anything But Love

In 1972, the veteran film comedienne Patsy Kelly was starring in the Broadway revival of No, No, Nanette. In 1927, less than two years after that show closed its first run, Miss Kelly introduced this song in Delmar's Revels, which ran just two weeks. But the following year it was interpolated in Lew Leslie's Blackbirds of 1928, and it has been a hit ever since, with over 450 different recordings and performances in at least nine movies.

Words by: Dorothy Fields      Music by: Jimmy McHugh

# S'POSIN'

**Words by: Andy Razaf**

**Music by: Paul Denniker**

"S'posin'" is a 1929 collaboration between Razaf, who wrote the lyrics to some of Fats Waller's most famous songs (including "Honeysuckle Rose," "Ain't Misbehavin'" and "Keepin' Out of Mischief Now"), and Denniker, pianist and arranger with Will Osborne's band and creator—with Razaf—of "Milkman's Matinee" and

"Make Believe Ballroom." Razaf, whose full name is Andreamenentania Razafinkeriefo, is the nephew of Ranavalona III, the last Queen of Madagascar, and the son of the Grand Duke of Madagascar. When the Duke was killed fighting the French invasion of the island in 1896, his widow fled to Washington, where Andy was born.

# Who's Sorry Now?

**Words by: Bert Kalmar and Harry Ruby**
**Music by: Ted Snyder**

*There has never been a generation gap where this song was concerned. Written specifically for the vaudeville team of Crafts and Haley, it was taken over by the biggest team of all—Van and Schenck—to become one of the top hits of 1923. About 35 years later a young rock singer, Connie Francis, was looking for a song to launch her career. Her father remembered this hit and suggested she sing it against a strong rock beat. By early '58 her record was No. 1 on the charts.*

# Three O'Clock in the Morning

It has become traditional for dance bands to play an unmistakable, even mandatory, "goodnight" theme at the close of a dance evening. "Three O'Clock in the Morning" is such a song. But even without such theme use, the tune has been one of the most popular waltzes since the Strauss era. Our version—with lyrics—was introduced in a review, Greenwich Follies of 1921.

**Words by: Dorothy Terriss**
**Music by: Julian Robledo**

It's Three O'- clock In The Morn - ing,
We've danced the whole night thru,_____ And day-light
soon will be dawn - ing, Just one more waltz with

One portion of this song's lyrics has required updating three times—the lines referring to a current long-running show. In the original version (1925) the long-run record holder was Abie's Irish Rose.

**Words by: Lorenz Hart**

Later, new lyrics referred to South Pacific. Then came a version that celebrated My Fair Lady. For the latest edition the publisher picked the successful but controversial all-nude Oh! Calcutta!

**Music by: Richard Rodgers**

# MANHATTAN

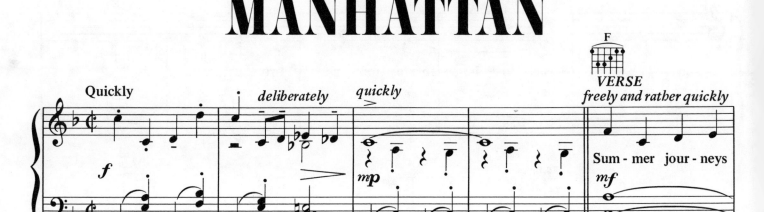

old Man - hat - tan, We'll set - tle down right here in town:

**CHORUS**
**Moderately, in tempo**

We'll have Man - hat - tan,
We'll go to Green - wich,

The Bronx and Stat - en Is - land too;
Where mod - ern men itch To be free;

It's love - ly go - ing through the Zoo;
And Bowl - ing Green you'll see with me;

*simile*

It's ver - y fan - cy On old De - lan - cey
We'll bathe at Bright - on The fish you'll fright - en

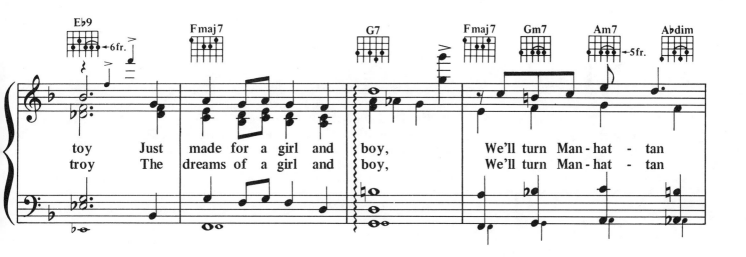

toy    Just made for a girl and boy, We'll turn Man - hat - tan
troy    The dreams of a girl and boy, We'll turn Man - hat - tan

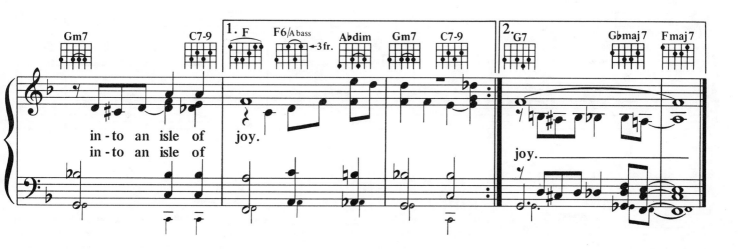

in - to an isle of joy.
in - to an isle of joy._____

We'll go to Yonkers
Where true love conquers
In the wilds;
And starve together, dear, in Childs'
We'll go to Coney
And eat bologny on a roll;
In Central Park, we'll stroll
Where our first kiss we stole,
Soul to soul;
\* Though "Oh! Calcutta!" has raised a flutter on Broadway
We both may see it clothed some day;
The city's clamor can never spoil
The dreams of a boy and goil
We'll turn Manhattan Into an isle of joy.

     \* Original Lyric: *Our future babies we'll take to "Abie's Irish Rose."*
                   *I hope they'll live to see it close.*
     First Revision: *And "South Pacific" is a terrific show they say:*
                   *We both may see it close some day.*
  Second Revision: *And for some high fare we'll go to "My Fair Lady" say,*
                   *We'll hope to see it close some day.*

# My Blue Heaven

In the 1920s everyone knew the name of Irving Berlin, but few people outside the music business knew the name of his closest song-writing rival—Walter Donaldson. In 1927, the year when Berlin's hit "Blue Skies" overshadowed most others, Donaldson's similarly tinted "My Blue Heaven," written three years before, burst out as the biggest hit so far in the century. Although sales records have been lost, it is estimated that Gene Austin's recording of the song sold more than 12 million copies.

**Words by: George Whiting**          **Music by: Walter Donaldson**

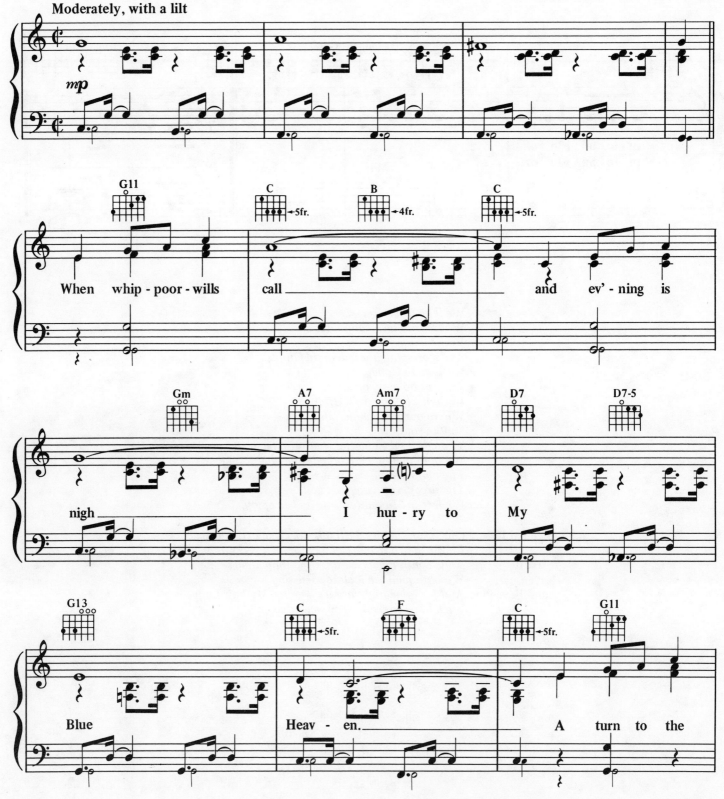

# Raindrops Keep Fallin' on My Head

*The rhythms, language and even the eccentric moods of the '60s and '70s dance forth from every phrase of the many hits of Bacharach and David. When "Raindrops" is sung off-screen in Butch Cassidy and the Sundance Kid, you know all about the characters and their feelings, even though the words have nothing at all to do with the on-screen action. The song won the Academy's Oscar for the Best Film Song of 1969.*

**Words by: Hal David**             **Music by: Burt Bacharach**

# Call Me Irresponsible

*When Cahn and Van Heusen wrote this song—in 1955—it was for Fred Astaire to sing in a film entitled* Papa's Delicate Condition. *But Paramount didn't get around to making the picture until 1963, with Jackie Gleason instead of Astaire. The song was inserted at the last minute and won the Academy Award. It was a record hit for both Frank Sinatra and Jack Jones.*

**Words by: Sammy Cahn**
**Music by: James Van Heusen**

# MOON RIVER

*For Breakfast at Tiffany's, Mercer and Mancini wrote this wistful tune to be sung by wistful Holly Golightly (Audrey Hepburn). Mercer's original title was "Blue River," but he discovered an earlier, unsuccessful song by that name, composed by a friend. Rather than risk offending anyone, he changed the word "Blue" to "Moon." The effect was magical, and "Moon River," despite the concurrent rage for rock 'n' roll, won the Academy Award as Best Film Song of 1961.*

**Words by: Johnny Mercer**          **Music by: Henry Mancini**

# ALFIE

Michael Caine starred in the British film Alfie as an irresponsible philanderer whose charm could never quite disguise the desperation of his own moral blindness. Musical scores for films are usually added after the picture has been shot, and most of the music for Alfie was improvised to the on-screen action by jazz saxophonist Sonny Rollins. But one song was needed at the end of the story to sum up the central character. Lyricist David read the script in his Long Island home while composer Bacharach flew to California to see a "rough cut" of the film. They conferred by phone and Hal wrote the lyric that, in his words, "put a button on the picture." P.S.: Hal David never did see the picture until it played in his neighborhood movie house.

Words by: Hal David
Music by: Burt Bacharach

on - ly fools are kind,    Al - fie,__    then I  guess it is wise to be

cruel.    And if  life be - longs    on - ly to the    strong, Al - fie,    What

will  you lend  on an old    gold - en rule?    As    sure    as I  be -

lieve    there's a  heav - en a - bove,    Al - fie,    I

know    there's some - thing much    more.    Some - thing e - ven    non - be - liev - ers

can be-lieve in.    I be-lieve in love,    Al-fie.

With-out true love we just ex-ist,    Al-fie.    Un-til you find the love you've

missed you're noth-ing,    Al-fie.    When you walk let your heart    lead the way    and

you'll find love an-y day,    Al-fie,    Al-fie.

*gradually getting softer*

148

# I Will Wait for You

*When the French film* Umbrellas of Cherbourg *became a "sleeper" hit on the art-film circuit, much of the credit went to the melodious, mood-spinning score by the talented Legrand. Gimbel learned about this song—part of the score—from a French colleague. By the time the rights were assigned to an American publisher, he had finished this lyric.*

**English Words by: Norman Gimbel**  **Music by: Michel Legrand**

INTERLUDE
Moderate swing tempo

150

Straight to my wait-ing arms.

(No chord) *Tempo I*

If it takes for-ev-er I Will Wait For You, For a thou-sand sum-mers I Will Wait For You, 'Til you're here be-side me, 'til I'm touch-ing you And for-ev-er more shar-ing your love.

# Hi-Lili, Hi-Lo

Composer Kaper, Polish-born, is a conservatory-trained musician, the creator of dozens of impressive film scores and a handful of top hits. Miss Deutsch is a writer of screen plays with such credits as National Velvet, King Solomon's Mines, Golden Earrings *and* Lili. *It was for the last-named that she turned lyricist, supplying the delicious folklike words that match the happy-go-lucky feeling of this ingenuous Kaper melody. For his overall scoring of the film, Kaper won an Oscar in 1953, but it was this charming little waltz tune, as sung by petite Leslie Caron, that won the hearts of millions of moviegoers, young and old alike.*

Words by:
**Helen Deutsch**

Music by:
**Bronislau Kaper**

# Mona Lisa

In 1949 songwriters Livingston and Evans were asked by Paramount to write a song for Captain Carey of the U.S.A., an Alan Ladd film about the O.S.S. in Italy during World War II—a warning song. Every time the Nazis were in the neighborhood, a strolling accordionist was to play this melody. "Mona Lisa" was the song, and it was given the Academy Award.

**Words and Music by: Jay Livingston and Ray Evans**

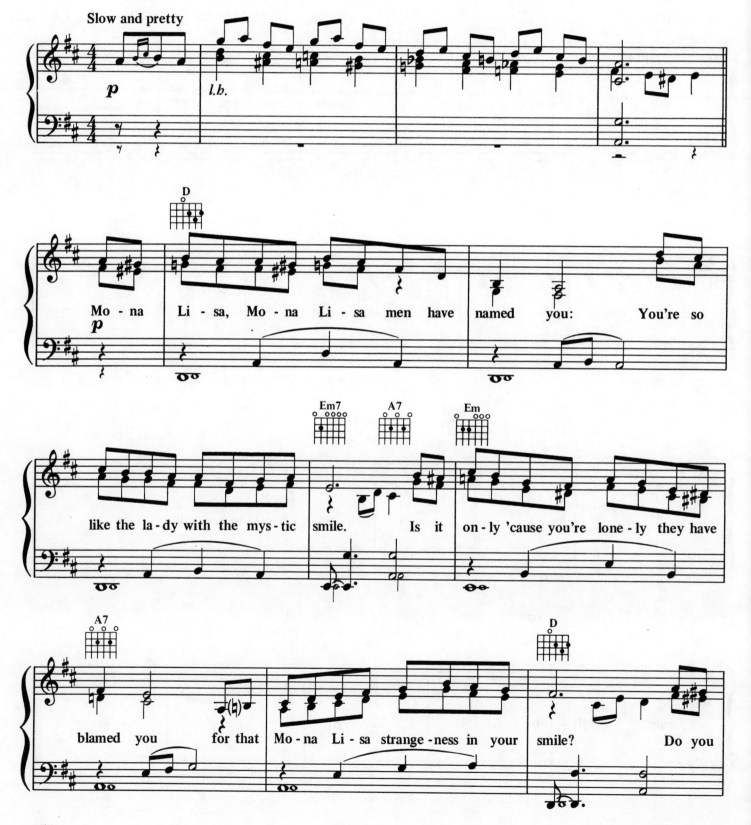

smile to tempt a lov-er, Mo-na Li-sa, Or is this your way to hide a brok-en

heart? Man-y dreams have been brought to your door-step. They just

lie there, and they die there. Are you warm, are you real, Mo-na

(No chords)

Li-sa, Or just a cold and lone-ly, love-ly work of art? Mo-na

*slower*

Li-sa, Mo-na Li-sa.

*pp*

# A Time for Us
## (Love Theme from *Romeo and Juliet*)

*Franco Zeffirelli's poetic filming of Romeo and Juliet in 1968
produced a love song that seemed to hark back to Eliza-
bethan, or even earlier, times. It was sung at the candlelit
ball when Romeo first caught sight of Juliet.*

**Words by: Larry Kusik and
Eddie Snyder
Music by: Nino Rota**

Time ___ For Us ___ at last ___ to see ___ A life ___ worth-
while ___ for you ___ and me. And with our love through tears and
thorns we will en- dure as we pass sure - ly through ev-'ry storm. A Time For
Us, some - day there'll be ___ a new world; ___ A
world of shin-ing hope for you and me.

# LOVER

Words by: Lorenz Hart

Music by: Richard Rodgers

*Some of the most exhilarating, melodious waltzes since the heyday of the Strauss family have been composed right here in North America by Richard Rodgers. These include "Falling in Love with Love," "The Carousel Waltzes" and—the first of his big waltz hits—"Lover," a favorite of musicians because of its sophisticated chromatic melody and harmonic progression. It was composed for a Jeanette MacDonald-Maurice Chevalier film of 1932—Love Me Tonight.*

160

# Louise

In 1929, for the first time, Hollywood films produced more hit songs than the Broadway stage. The era of big Hollywood Musicals exploded with such hit-producing vehicles as Hollywood Revue of 1929, Broadway Melody, Love Parade, Gold Diggers of Broadway, On with the Show, The Vagabond Lover, Sunny Side Up, and Maurice Chevalier's American debut film Innocents of Paris. The Frenchman's smashing success with the American public was assured when he sang this new "name" song. When the decade began, our musical flame was "Margie" (page 188), but when it closed, all North America was serenading a new sweetheart—"Louise."

**Words by: Leo Robin**
**Music by: Richard A. Whiting**

(No chords)

Ev-'ry lit-tle breeze seems to whis-per "Lou-ise." Birds in the trees— seem to
*light and gay*

twit-ter "Lou-ise." Each lit-tle rose— Tells me it knows— I

love you, love you. Ev-'ry lit-tle beat that I feel in my heart,—

Seems to re-peat— What I felt at the start.— Each lit-tle sigh—

Tells me that I— a-dore you,— Lou-ise Just to see and

# Laura

To promote a movie, a title song is often added to the sound track. When Laura, a suspense thriller, opened in 1944, it had only a background theme that recurred to identify the central character. Unexpectedly, audiences went wild over Raksin's untitled music, and Twentieth Century-Fox's music firm quickly commissioned Mercer to write appropriate lyrics. Some months later, Woody Herman's recording made "Laura" a million-seller.

**Words by: Johnny Mercer**          **Music by: David Raksin**

165

# Pennies from Heaven

A storm was crashing outside; inside the ramshackle house Bing Crosby, accompanying himself on an ancient lute, sang "Pennies from Heaven" to lull little Edith Fellows to sleep. The scene took place in the film of the same name in which Louis Armstrong also appeared, and both Bing and "Satchmo" have been identified with the song ever since. The film also marked the beginning of a 20-year association between Crosby and lyricist Burke. During this period Burke turned out hit after hit with such collaborators as Johnston ("The Moon Got in My Eyes" and "One, Two, Button Your Shoe" as well as "Pennies from Heaven"), Jimmie Monaco ("I've Got a Pocketful of Dreams," "An Apple for the Teacher") Jimmy Van Heusen ("Polka Dots and Moonbeams," "Imagination" and the Oscar-winning "Swinging on a Star").

**Words by: John Burke**          **Music by: Arthur Johnston**

168

# Pass Me By

**Words by:**
Carolyn Leigh

**Music by:**
Cy Coleman

*Early in his career, Cary Grant (he was known then as Archie Leach) was a performer in English music halls. Years later, when planning his picture Father Goose, he asked for a main musical theme in the vein of those old music hall songs. Composer Coleman recalls that Grant would sing some of these in his ear while they were lunching with a table full of Hollywood executives. But the inspiration eluded Cy for two weeks until one day he was walking with the star and stopped to talk with a friend. Grant walked on ahead and Cy noticed "the jaunty, jolly way that he walked." He took his tempo and rhythm from that walk and then realized that these were right in step with Grant's music hall ditties. He completed the tune that same afternoon, put in a phone call to lyricist Leigh in New York, and the result was this "jaunty, jolly" march song.*

mand. A liv-e-ly pair of heels that kick to beat the

band. Con - tem - plat - in'

(No chord) na - ture can be fas - ci - nat - in'. Add to these a

nose that I can thumb, And a mouth by

gum have I,_____ To tell the whole darn

# Theme from
# LOVE STORY
## (Where Do I Begin)

*The phenomenal success of Erich Segal's Love Story, both as a book and as a movie, demonstrated that the rock (and roll)-ribbed world still welcomes old-fashioned sentiment and even pathos. When the film hit in 1970, the very pianistic, almost Mozartean theme music became the biggest seller of the year. It should be a symbol of young love for years to come.*

**Words by: Carl Sigman**  **Music by: Francis Lai**

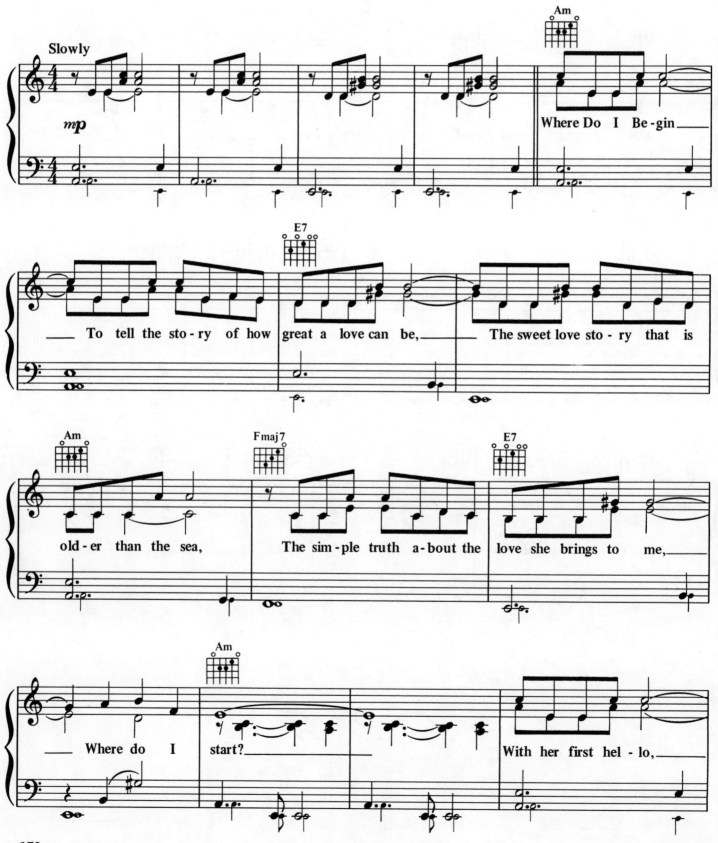

# MORE

When the controversial Italian film Mondo Cane (A Dog's World) was first shown in the United States, Ortolani's rich theme was heard only instrumentally. But after an English writer, Newell, added lyrics, a complete vocal version was dubbed into the sound track. The vocalist was Ortolani's wife, the Italian star Katyna Ranieri. Actually, the purely romantic song had nothing to do with the premise of the film, which was a study of bizarre, often unappetizing, social behavior. Today the film is all but forgotten, but "More" has become one of our most-performed perennials and a big favorite at weddings, threatening to displace "Oh, Promise Me." It won the Grammy Award for the best instrumental theme of 1963 and has been recorded by more than 400 different artists.

**English Words by: Norman Newell**          **Italian Words by: M. Ciorciolini**

**Music by: R. Ortolani and N. Oliviero**

176

# For Me and My Gal

*In 1917, according to composer Meyer, "I was writing songs for a living and I needed money, so I wrote this ballad." Leslie borrowed the title from the last line of that earlier hit, "Shine on Harvest Moon." When first introduced in vaudeville it "laid an egg," until the legendary songplugger Max Winslow placed it with such hit-makers as Al Jolson, Sophie Tucker, Eddie Cantor and George Jessel. In 1942 it served as the title song of a movie starring Gene Kelly (his first) and Judy Garland, and it became a hit all over again.*

**Words by: Edgar Leslie and E. Ray Goetz**

**Music by: George W. Meyer**

The par-son's wait - ing For Me And My

Gal. And some-time I'm gon-na build a lit-tle

home for two, For three or four or more In

love - land For Me And My Gal.

(For Me And My Gal!)

# Cruising Down the River
## (On a Sunday Afternoon)

*Two middle-aged lady musicians wrote this to win a British songwriting contest in 1945. It achieved worldwide fame in World War II when H.M.S. Amethyst made its historic dash down the Yangtze—the crew sang this song as they defied Chinese guns. In the U.S.A. both Blue Barron and Russ Morgan recorded million-selling versions.*

By: Eily Beadell
and
Nell Tollerton

The old ac - cord - ion play - ing

A sen - ti - men - tal tune

Cruis - ing Down The Riv - er on a Sun - day

af - ter - noon. The birds a - bove all

sing of love A gen - tle sweet re - frain

# Let Me Call You Sweetheart
## (I'm in Love with You)

**Words by: Beth Slater Whitson**

**Music by: Leo Friedman**

*Illinois-born Friedman (1869–1927) was the composer of popular instrumental "reveries," "Indian" novelties and cakewalks in the turn-of-the-century mold. Mrs. Whitson (1879–1930) was a poetess from Tennessee whose verses appeared in magazines. In 1909 they collaborated on "Meet Me Tonight in Dreamland," which they sold outright for a small fee to a publisher, only to watch it sell 2 million copies of sheet music. The following year they wrote "Sweetheart," which sold 5 million, but this time they had been shrewd enough to make a contract for royalties on every copy sold.*

love        me        too.

Keep      the     love - light   glow - ing        in       your

eyes        so        true.

Let      Me      Call      You      Sweet - heart,      I'm      in

love        with        you.

"Heart of My Heart, I Love You So" was just a line in "The Story of a Rose," a hit song of 1899 which, as "Heart of My Heart," endured for years as a favorite with barbershop

# The Gang That Sang
# "Heart of My Heart"

**Words and Music by: Ben Ryan**

quartets. A quarter of a century later, Ryan capitalized on its lasting popularity by writing another song about singing that old favorite. It proved to be as popular as the original.

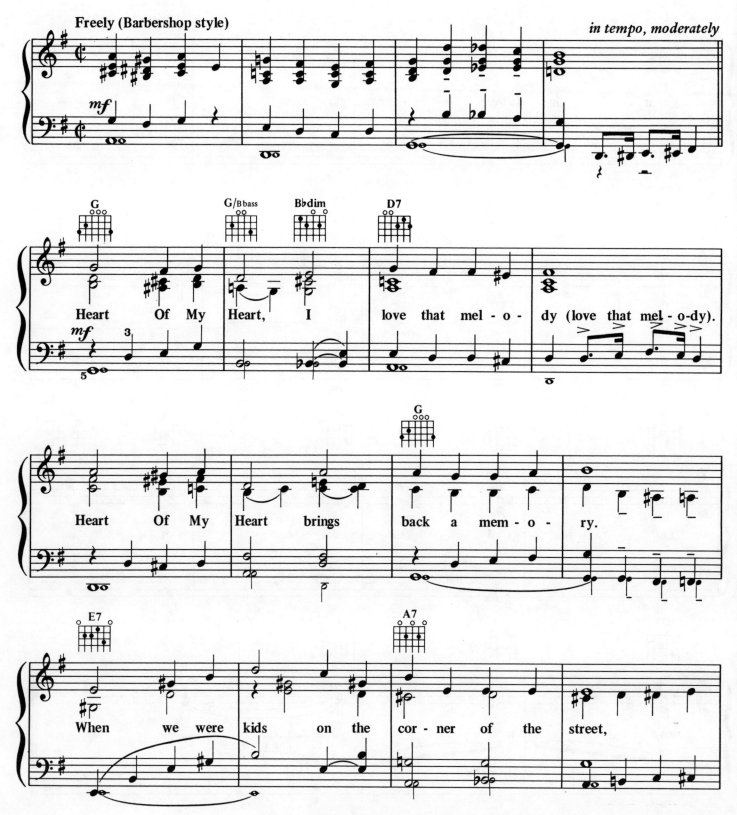

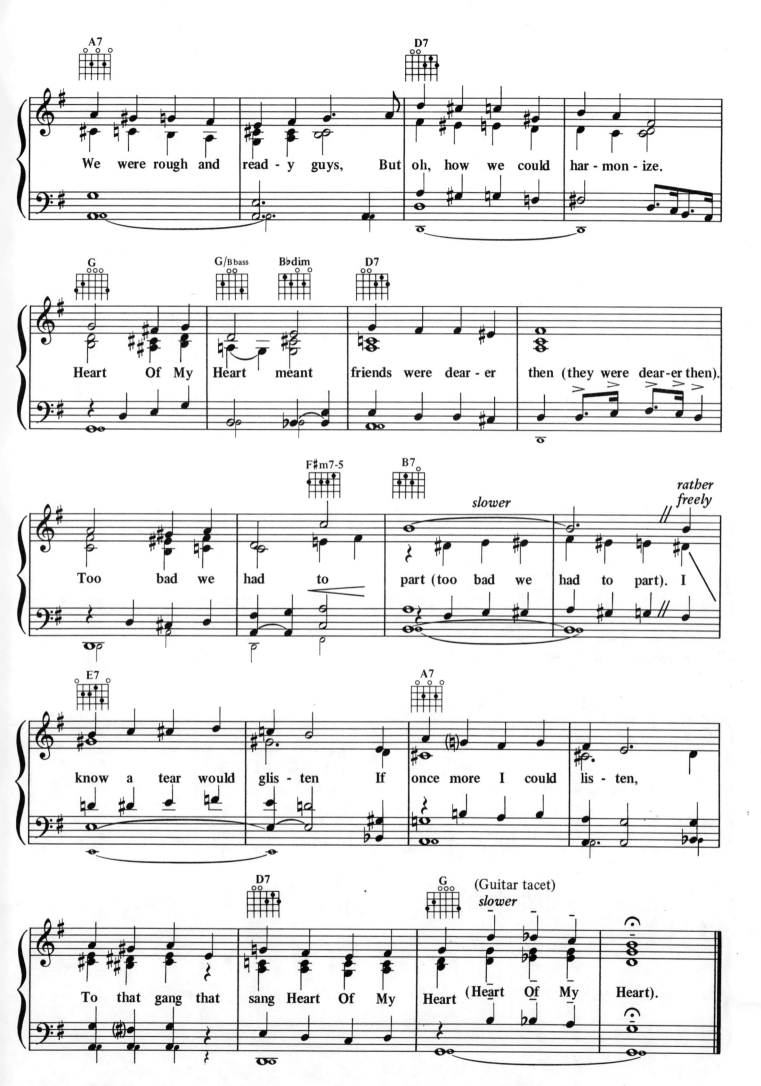

# Margie

Robinson was pianist with the Original Dixieland Jazz Band and "Margie" was the band's biggest record. But its greater popularity is due to Eddie Cantor, who sang it for his daughter Marjorie in his revue, The Midnight Rounders of 1921. "Margie" was the second Cantor female thus celebrated. Earlier Cantor had appropriated the old tune "Ida, Sweet as Apple Cider" for his wife.

Words by: Benny Davis          Music by: Con Conrad and J. Russel Robinson

My lit-tle Mar - gie, I'm al-ways think-ing of you, Mar - gie, I'll tell the world I love you, Don't for - get your prom-ise to me,

# The Sweetheart of Sigma Chi

Words by:
Byron D. Stokes

Music by:
F. Dudleigh Vernor

The most popular of all fraternity songs was born in 1912 on the campus of Albion College in Michigan. Vernor was practicing on the chapel organ when Stokes handed him the words. In the space of one hour he composed the tune. Of course the writers and their fraternity brothers sang it, and its fame spread around the campus. Vernor and his "brother" printed 500 copies of the song, sending one to each Sigma Chi chapter. Orders flooded in, the writers turned the song over to a major publisher, and in no time all the world was serenading "The Sweetheart of Sigma Chi."

Fades in the af - ter - glow._____ The

blue of her eyes and the gold of her hair Are a

blend of the west - ern sky;_____ And the

moon - light beams On the girl of my dreams, She's The

Sweet - heart Of Sig - ma Chi.

# The Whiffenpoof Song

## (Baa! Baa! Baa!)

One of Yale's most cherished traditions—this song—was probably composed by a Harvard man! Guy Scull is believed to have set this melody in the '90s to a freely adapted version of Kipling's poem titled "Gentlemen Rankers." In 1909, The Whiffenpoofs, an offshoot of the Yale Glee Club, was organized, taking its name from an imaginary fish out of Victor Herbert's operetta Little Nemo. In that same year, Whiffenpoofers Minnigerode, Pomeroy and Galloway altered Kipling's words and Scull's music. The song was altered again slightly in 1935 when a 1927 Yale grad, Rudy Vallee, decided to popularize it through his radio program and recording.

**Words and Music by: Meade Minnigerode,
George S. Pomeroy, Tod B. Galloway
Revision by: Rudy Vallee**

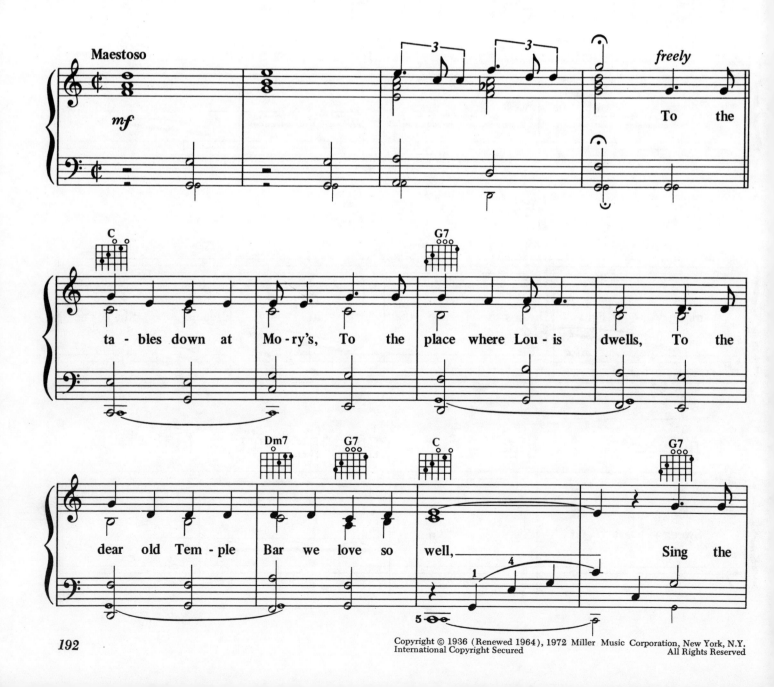

To the ta-bles down at Mo-ry's, To the place where Lou-is dwells, To the dear old Tem-ple Bar we love so well, Sing the

193

**Words and
Music by:
Bob Carleton**

Old-timers tend to look down upon the latter-day variety of nonsense ditties. But the generations that frowned on "Three Little Fishies" and "Mairzy Doats" once had a ball singing and dancing to "Barney Google," "YES! We Have No Bananas" and, before that, during World War I, to the lively, lilting "Ja-Da," written as a take-off on the pseudo-Oriental songs popular at that time. ("Japanese Sandman" and "Hindustan" led the way.) On the serious side, musicologist Sigmund Spaeth saw in this gibberish song "a foretaste of modern Dadaism, Dali and Gertrude Stein." Although it would probably have gradually faded away as a popular tune, Dixieland bands took up "Ja-Da," finding it melodically and harmonically ideal for freewheeling collective improvisations, and it became established as part of the traditional Dixieland repertoire. And when the cha-cha rage hit in the '50s, the lyric became "Ja-Da Ja-Da Cha-Cha-Cha" as easily as it made the rythmic transition to the new Latin beat of the day.

# LAST NIGHT ON THE BACK PORCH

## (I Loved Her Best of All)

Carl Schraubstader wrote one unforgettable hit; then he turned his back on Tin Pan Alley forever, to become a businessman in New York City. "I went to high school with Richard Rodgers," he told the Digest, "and I knew I'd never be another Rodgers." He wrote this during his sophomore year at Cornell for the annual Masque Show. It became the campus favorite, and at house-party time all the bands were asked to play it. One of these was a bunch of kids from Penn State University. Their leader, Fred Waring, liked it enough to take it with him on his first big-time job in Pittsburgh. When the song was published, the great lyricist Lew Brown rewrote parts of the verse, but the chorus, which appears here, is pure Schraubstader.

**Words and Music by:**

**Lew Brown and Carl Schraubstader**

**[Taxi]**

I loved her in a Packard
And a Locomobile,
I loved her in a Buick
While she held on to the wheel.
I loved her in a flivver
And we ran into a wall,
But last night in a taxi
I loved her best of all.

**[Moonshine]**

I loved her in a rainstorm
And I loved her in snow,
I loved her in a blizzard
When zero was below.
I loved her in the sunshine
Underneath her parasol,
But last night with some moonshine
I loved her best of all.

**[Leap Year]**

From Monday until Sunday
Oh! I sure am some sheik,
I love her, yes! I love her
Ev'ry day that's in the week.
Tho' seven days of Heaven
Ain't enough I won't get sore,
'Cause next year when it's leap year
I'll love her one day more.

**[In between time]**

I loved her at breakfast
And I loved her at tea,
I loved her yes! I loved her
When she took her lunch with me.
I loved her after supper
When I paid her folks a call,
But last night in between time
I loved her best of all.

**[Rowboat]**

I loved her in a sailboat
And a big birch canoe,
I loved her on a tugboat
And an ocean liner too.
I loved her in a schooner
And I loved her in a yawl,
But last night in a rowboat
I loved her best of all.

**[College]**

I loved her in the classroom
In Latin and Greek,
I loved her in Italian
That's a language she can't speak.
I loved her on the campus
And in the dining hall,
But last night at the junior prom
I loved her best of all.

# Show Me the Way to Go Home

Since it was first published in 1925, this theme has been used by dance bands as the none-too-subtle signal that "the party's over." There have been many songs with a similar message, even similar lines, but none that has managed to convey the damp, convivial mood of an evening's end so succinctly and harmoniously. Irving King was actually a pseudonym—the song was the first collaboration of the British writers and publishers Jimmy Campbell and Reg Connelly, who founded their successful London firm with it. Six years later they collaborated with orchestra leader Ray Noble to compose that other and more romantic "closer," "Goodnight Sweetheart" (page 44).

Words and Music by:
**Irving King**

Moderately, with a steady beat

Show Me The Way To Go Home, I'm tired and I want to go to bed, I had a lit-tle drink a-bout an hour a-go, And it's

# YES! We Have No Bananas

By: Frank Silver
and
Irving Cohn

The writers purportedly wrote this concoction after hearing the phrase from a Greek fruit peddler, but, according to Sigmund Spaeth, its melody borrowed, consciously or unconsciously, from Handel's "Hallelujah Chorus," "My Bonnie," "I Dreamt That I Dwelt in Marble Halls," "Aunt Dinah's Quilting Party" and Cole Porter's "An Old-Fashioned Garden." Substituting the original lyrics from those to the appropriate melodic phrases you get: "Hallelujah, Bananas! Oh, bring back my Bonnie to me. I dreamt that I dwelt in marble halls—the king that you seldom see. I was seeing Nellie home, to an old-fashioned garden: but, Hallelujah, Bananas! Oh, bring back my Bonnie to me!"

Moderately bright

YES! We Have No Ba - na - nas, We have no ba - na - nas to - day. We've string beans and HON - ions, cab - BAH - ges and scal - lions, And

# Alice Blue Gown

In 1919 the fashions favored a shade of light blue which was dominant in the wardrobe of Alice Roosevelt Longworth, daughter of Teddy Roosevelt. This topical note was played by Tierney and McCarthy in their first musical, Irene, Broadway's biggest hit up to that time. (It played 670 performances and sent 17 companies on the road!) On stage, this lovely waltz tune was sung by Irene, assistant and model to a fashionable dressmaker. As is the way in such Cinderella-like plots, Irene inevitably marries a millionaire.

**Words by:**
Joseph McCarthy

**Music by:**
Harry Tierney

In my sweet lit-tle A-lice Blue Gown,_____ When I first wan-dered down in to town,_____ I was both proud and

# HARRIGAN

**Words and Music
by:
George M. Cohan**

*For his 1907 show,* The Talk of the Town, *Cohan wrote a "spelling hit," "When We Are M-A-Double R-I-E-D." But the following year the formula was even more successful with "H-A-Double R-I-G-A-N." The show this time was* Fifty Miles from Boston; *Boston being, then as now, the Irish capital of North America. "Harrigan" became a new Irish rallying cry—an anthem in a class with Cohan's own "Give My Regards to Broadway," "I'm a Yankee Doodle Dandy" and—much later—"Over There." It was typically Cohan's way of saying he was "proud of all the Irish blood that's in me." Cohan was a performer, producer and director as well as a writer and composer. He died in his sleep at the age of 64 in 1942, the same year Jimmy Cagney portrayed him and sang "Harrigan" in his filmed biography,* Yankee Doodle Dandy. *At Cohan's funeral, held in New York's St. Patrick's Cathedral, "Over There," played as a dirge, became the first popular song ever heard in the cathedral.*

# NOTRE DAME VICTORY MARCH

*America's best-known college victory march was composed in 1908, many years before victory became a habit for*

*Notre Dame football teams. The first performance was on the organ of the college's Sacred Heart Church.*

Words by:
**John F. Shea**

Music by:
**Rev. Michael J. Shea**

Cheer! Cheer for old No - tre Dame.

Wake up the ech - oes cheer - ing her name.

Send the vol - ley cheer on high;

# Beer Barrel Polka
## (Roll out the Barrel)

Translated from Czech, its original title was "Unrequited Love," hardly suitable for the merriest, most popular polka of all time. But in 1939, the American labels for a German recording carried the present title. At that time, any mention of liquor on radio was taboo, but the juke box business had begun to roll, and in no time at all, the song could be heard from every box in every tavern in the land.

By: Lew Brown,
Wladimir A. Timm,
Vasek Zeman and Jaromir Vejvoda

There's a gar-den, what a gar-den, on-ly hap-py fa-ces bloom there And there's nev-er an-y room there for a wor-ry or a

210

gloom there Oh there's mu-sic and there's dan-cing and a lot of sweet ro-

man-cing When they play a pol-ka they all get in the swing

Ev-'ry time they hear_____ that oom-pa- pa_____

_____ Ev-'ry-bo-dy feels_____ so tra-la- la_____

_____ They want to throw their cares a-way_____

They all go lah - de - ah - de - ay.

Then they hear a rum - ble on the floor

It's the big sur - prise they're wait - ing for

And all the cou - ples form a ring

For miles a - round you'll hear them sing:

212

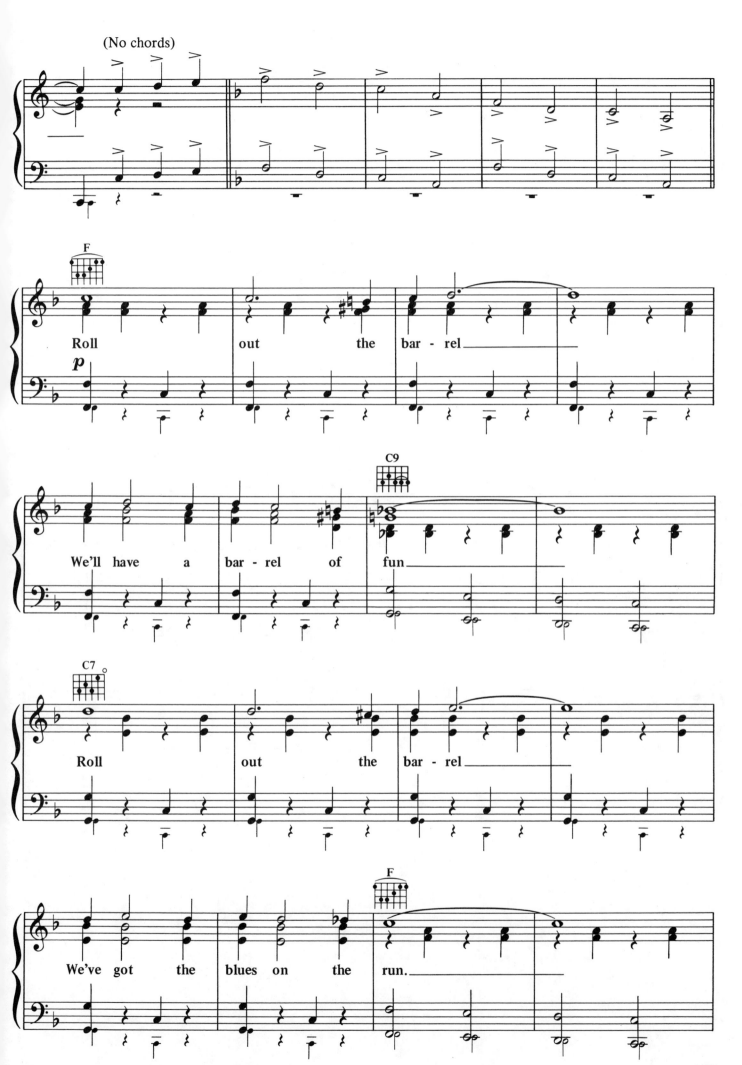

(No chords)

**F**

Roll out the bar - rel

*p*

We'll have a bar - rel of fun

**C9**

**C7**

Roll out the bar - rel

**F**

We've got the blues on the run.

Zing boom ta - rar - rel
*get louder gradually*

Ring out a song of good cheer

Now's the time to roll the bar - rel for the

gang's all here.

# Toyland

*Early in 1903 a musical version of* The Wonderful Wizard of Oz *had captivated both the young and the young-in-heart. For an immediate follow-up for the same "family trade" the producers asked Herbert to compose the score.* Babes in Toyland *was one of his biggest hits, and "Toyland" its most enduring delight.*

**Words by: Glen MacDonough**     **Music by: Victor Herbert**

Toy - land, Toy - land, Lit - tle girl and boy land,

While you dwell with - in it____ You are ev - er hap - py then.

Child - hood's joy - land, Mys - tic, mer - ry Toy - land!

Once you pass its bor - ders You can ne'er__ re - turn a - gain.____

*Note: Guitarists tune lowest string ½ tone higher to F.

# Santa Claus Is Comin' to Town

*This first of the big Christmas pop songs had rough sledding at first—publisher after publisher turned it down. Coots, who was writing special material for Eddie Cantor's radio shows, asked the star to introduce it, but Cantor felt it unsuitable for an adult audience. But his wife, Ida, persuaded him to sing it just before Thanksgiving in 1934. The song was an instant hit.*

Words and Music by:
**J. Fred Coots and Haven Gillespie**

Moderately, with a lilt · No guitar chords · *mp throughout* · Organ: No pedal

You bet-ter watch out, you bet-ter not cry, Bet-ter not pout, I'm tell-ing you why: San-ta Claus is com-in' to town.

He's mak-ing a list, and check-ing it twice, Gon-na find out who's naught-y and nice: San-ta Claus is com-in' to

# Beautiful Ohio

**Words by: Ballard MacDonald**
**Music by: Mary Earl**

In 1918, after the F. W. Woolworth chain had sold 100,000 copies of this hit, the publisher, Shapiro, Bernstein, decided to raise its wholesale price from 8¢ to 18¢ per copy —an unheard-of amount in those days. But public demand for the song swept away all resistance and it went on to sell more than 5 million copies. The composer, Robert A. King, who used the pseudonym of Mary Earl, was an employe of the publisher, under contract to write four songs a month, which were to become the outright property of the firm. Although under no obligation to do so, Shapiro, Bernstein eventually paid King $60,000 in royalties. In 1969, "Beautiful Ohio," a tribute to both a river and a state, became the official state song of Ohio.

# Ma (He's Making Eyes at Me)

*Vaudeville was the entertainment firmament in 1921, and Eddie Cantor was one of its top stars. For a Shubert revue called* The Midnight Rounders, *the ebullient Cantor style cried out for a novelty number, preferably one which would give him a chance to roll those "saucer" eyes. Cantor's rendition of "Ma" helped keep the show running for two years.*

**Words by: Sidney Clare**

**Music by: Con Conrad**

# Wait Till the Sun Shines, Nellie

The idea for this song came to Von Tilzer in 1905 from a newspaper item reporting a fire in which only the father and youngest child in a family were saved. The father accepted his tragedy as a deal of Fate which was certain to be followed by a spell of happiness. Von Tilzer abstracted the optimistic notion and constructed a new story line about two lovers whose plans for a Sunday together are frustrated by bad weather.

Words by:
Andrew B. Sterling

Music by:
Harry Von Tilzer

*Note: Both melody and bass may be played in octaves.

# I Walk the Line

*While Johnny Cash was in the Air Force, stationed in Germany, he discovered that someone had been fooling with his tape recorder. When he turned it on a weird melody sounded. This stayed in his head for months. Then one day he happened to play the tape "backwards" and discovered that it actually was somebody practicing a series of guitar runs. He started practicing the same runs, in between chanting that backwards melody to the words, "Because you're mine I walk the line." The song grew gradually, was recorded and gave Cash his first million-seller, a theme song and international fame.*

**Words and Music by: John R. Cash**

Moderately bright country tempo

*mp*
*(bring out the bass)*

I keep a close watch on this heart of mine.
ver - y, ver - y eas - y to be true.

I keep my eyes wide o - pen all the time.
I find my - self a - lone when each day is through.

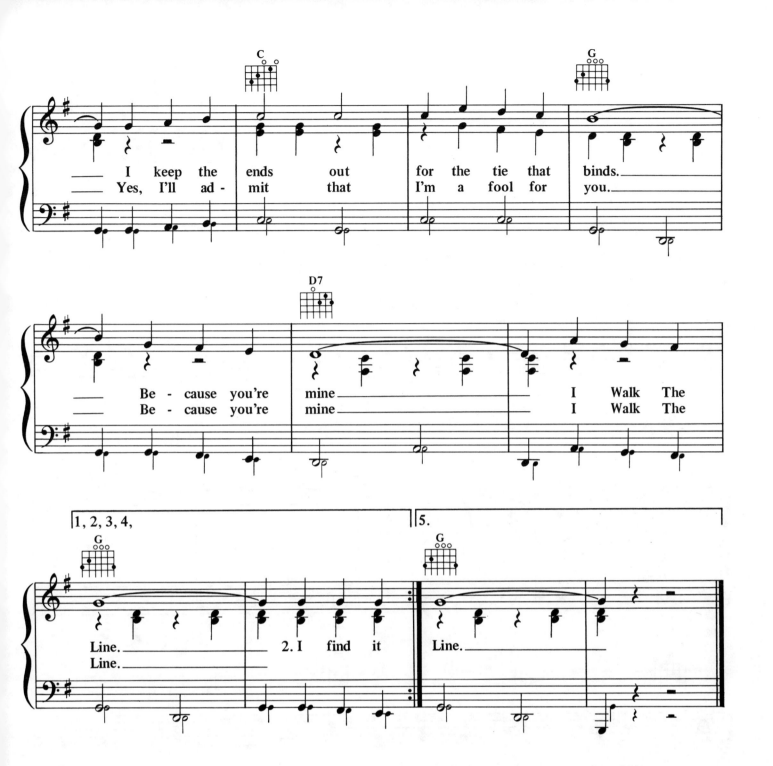

I keep the ends out for the tie that binds.____
Yes, I'll ad - mit out that I'm a fool for you.____

Be - cause you're mine____ I Walk The
Be - cause you're mine____ I Walk The

1, 2, 3, 4,

5.

Line.____ 2. I find it
Line.____

Line.____

# BOUQUET OF ROSES

One of the biggest country hits of all time was written by two city "fellers"—in a New York recording studio! When Nelson sang the melody to Hilliard, a comment that the melody was "flowery" led to the subject of roses, but for the sake of freshness this ordinarily romantic subject was given a reverse twist.

**Words and Music by:**
**Steve Nelson**
**and**
**Bob Hilliard**

# Wildwood Flower

No one can be sure when this flower of a song began to bloom—
it could be several hundred years old. But it seems to have hidden
away among the Appalachian mountains until the late A. P. Carter
transplanted it to the main furrow of country- and folk-music con-
sciousness. Its sweet, mournful theme is in the purest country tradition, so it's easy to understand how the Carter Family's recording, in 1928, captured an almost universal audience. Mother
Maybelle's guitar pickin' on that disc set a new style and standard
for the field. Today virtually every country star, including the
latter-day Carters—Anita, June and Helen (and June's husband
Johnny Cash)—has his or her own special version of the song.

**Traditional**

2. Oh, he promised to love me, he promised to love;
   And to cherish me always all others above.
   I woke from my dream and my idol was clay;
   My passion for loving had vanished away.

3. Oh, he taught me to love him; he called me his flower;
   A blossom to cheer him through life's weary hour.
   But now he is gone, he's left me alone;
   The wild flowers to weep and the wild birds to mourn.

4. I'll dance and I'll sing and my life shall be gay;
   I'll charm every heart in the crowd I survey.
   Though my heart now is breaking he never will know
   How his name makes me tremble, my pale cheeks to glow.

5. I'll dance and I'll sing and my heart will be gay,
   I'll banish this weeping, drive troubles away.
   I'll live yet to see that he'll rue this dark hour
   When he won and neglected this frail wildwood flower.

# I Almost Lost My Mind

In 1946, when blues artist Ivory Joe Hunter was performing at a club in Nashville, he stayed in a rooming house on the outskirts of town, where he became particularly friendly with Martha Spencer, a waitress, and her Pullman-porter husband. A few years later Joe returned to the same club and the same house, but Spencer was gone–the couple had separated. Martha told him, "When he first left me, I almost lost my mind." "You know," Joe told the *Digest*, "I went right to the piano and the whole song came to me all at once–that's how it goes when an idea is for real–and Martha wrote down the words while I sang them."

**Words and Music by: Ivory Joe Hunter**

Slow and bluesy

1. When_____ I lost my ba - by I Al - most_ Lost_ My Mind_
pass_____ a mil-lion peo - ple, I can't_ tell_ who_ I meet.

When_____ I lost my ba - by I
pass_____ a mil-lion peo - ple, I

230

3. *I went to see a gypsy*
   *And had my fortune read.*
   *I went to see a gypsy,*
   *And had my fortune read.*
   *I hung my head in sorrow* '
   *When she said what she said.*

4. *Well, I can tell you people,*
   *The news was not so good.*
   *Well I can tell you people,*
   *The news was not so good.*
   *She said your baby has quit you,*
   *This time she's gone—for good.*

# RING of FIRE

*Johnny Cash's love for the Carter Family developed when he was a boy in Oklahoma, soaking up all the country and folk music he could manage to hear. In the early '60s he recorded several songs written by June Carter, one of the three daughters of Mother Maybelle of the original A. P. Carter Family group. These included "The Matador," co-written with Johnny, and "Ring of Fire," which she co-authored with Merle Kilgore. Around that time when Cash became addicted to pep pills and tranquilizers, it was Mother Maybelle and her girls who helped him "walk the line" again. Finally, in 1968, the "ring of fire" enveloped June and Johnny and they were married. This song, now a real country classic, has been recorded by top stars in the pop, country, soul and folk fields, including Tom Jones, Ray Charles, Burl Ives, and, of course, both Johnny and June.*

By: Merle Kilgore and June Carter

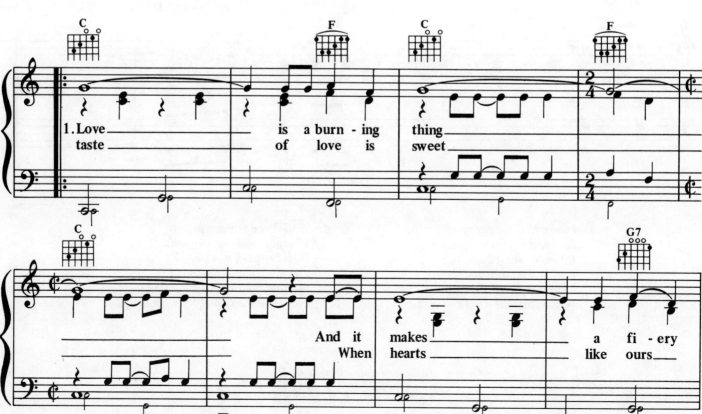

# Young at Heart

*When the late Nat Cole was introduced to Carolyn Leigh, his first words were "I goofed." He was referring to the fact that he had turned down this song a year before, dismissing it as one for the "geriatric set." In the interim, Frank Sinatra had made the definitive hit recording of it. Avant-garde arranger Richards wrote the melody, determined to produce a "commercial," singable hit. Several writers attempted lyrics, but none came up with a set to match the sunny mood of the tune until the publisher approached Miss Leigh. At the time her father, a man with a great zest for life, had become ill and depressed. "I wrote the words for him," she recalled for the* Digest, *"using some of his own philosophy to cheer him up. When the song became Number 1, he was the most happy fella in the hospital."*

**Words by: Carolyn Leigh**                    **Music by: Johnny Richards**

# Tenderly

The late Walter Gross, a marvelous pianist, wrote just one beautiful immortal hit. Most of the singers he accompanied in the '40s were familiar with "Walter's melody," but it remained untitled and unsung until singer Margaret Whiting introduced him to lyricist Lawrence. Lawrence recalls that Gross was reluctant to accept his title, feeling it sounded like directions to a performer. Today, when someone suggests, "Play Tenderly," you can be sure it's this song they have in mind.

**Words by: Jack Lawrence**
**Music by: Walter Gross**

239

# That's Amore
## (That's Love)

**Words by: Jack Brooks**

**Music by: Harry Warren**

Dean Martin has been indelibly associated with this American-Italian song ever since he introduced it in his 1953 film, The Caddy. Originally the movie's director wanted to use an old Neapolitan song like "Oi Marie" for an Italian family celebration scene, but composer Warren, himself of Italian descent, persuaded him to try a new "Italian" song. The result was the hit "That's Amore."

Bright and happy

When the moon hits your eye like a big piz - za pie, That's A - mor - e.

When the world seems to shine like you've had too much wine, That's A - mor - e.

When you dance down the street with a cloud at your feet, you're in love. ___ When you walk in a dream but you know you're not dream-ing, Sig-nor-e, ___ Scuz-za me, but you see, back in old Na-po-li, That's A-mor-e. ___

# The Breeze and I

*It began in 1929 as a piano piece called "Andaluza," part of the Andalucia Suite by the Cuban composer Lecuona. Stillman had been commissioned to write an "art song" lyric to the piece, but this went nowhere. Then, he recalls, he heard a now-forgotten dance band broadcast the melody in a fox-trot arrangement, and he saw the song in an entirely new light. Adapted to a standard 32-bar pop format, it ideally suited his lyric, "The Breeze and I." The composer and lyricist met only once. According to Stillman, "Lecuona didn't speak English and I didn't speak Spanish. We had a very short conversation."*

**Words by: Al Stillman**    **Music by: Ernesto Lecuona**

*Guitarists must tune lowest string to D.

244

245

# Autumn Leaves

This lovely, mood-inspiring song began as a French poem, "Les Feuilles Mortes," by Jacques Prévert. It was set to music by Hungarian-born Joseph Kosma and became a favorite among the better French café singers after World War II. Mercer, America's most prolific lyricist, was also, at that time, a busy recording executive and singer, but he loved the song and agreed to write the English lyrics. Then he became preoccupied with other matters. Reminded of his commitment, he hurriedly scribbled the lyrics in a cab on his way to a plane, stopping off enroute to slip them under the publisher's door. The song really hit its stride, however, in 1955 when a young pianist, Roger Williams, made a recording of a piano version which went on to sell 2½ million copies.

### Words and music by:

### Joseph Kosma, Jacques Prévert and Johnny Mercer

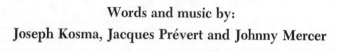

246

kiss - es_____ The sun-burned hands_____ I used to hold._____ Since you
went a - way_____ the days grow long_____ And soon I'll hear_____ old win-ter's
song_____ But I miss you most of all my dar - ling_____ When
Au - tumn Leaves start to fall.

# Blue Tango

In the 20-odd years of radio's Hit Parade only one instrumental selection made the No. 1 spot. (Lyrics were added immediately by the prolific Mitchell Parish, who had performed the same stunt for "Star Dust," "Deep Purple" and "Moonlight Serenade.") The composer of this phenomenon was a onetime music teacher at Radcliffe College, director of the Harvard Band, and house composer-arranger for the Boston Pops Orchestra. Each of Anderson's pieces for the Pops was a miniature tone poem with a decidedly popular appeal—"Blue Tango," for example, because of its contagious rhythm and the sly bit of fun that the song poked at the deep-dipping dance style of a generation ago.

**Words by: Mitchell Parish**

**Music by: Leroy Anderson**

248

press the de-sire— we used to know———— not long a - go. So just

hold me tight———— in your arms to - night,———

——————— and this Blue Tan-go will be our thrill - ing mem-o-ry of

love.

# Arrivederci, Roma

*Vienna has its song, "Vienna, City of My Dreams," for instant and enduring nostalgia. The same depth of feeling for a city was struck by the Italian writer-actor-entertainer Renato Rascel in 1954 with "Arrivederci, Roma" which means "Good-bye to Rome," but a "good-bye" that says "I will see you again." In a very short time this became the best-known, best-loved song about the Eternal City, one that brings a tear to the eye of any old or young Roman, to every tourist who ever has luxuriated in its ancient and modern splendor. Much of its success in North America is due to the English lyrics by the prolific Carl Sigman which capture completely the images and feeling of the Italian original. These were sung by Mario Lanza in his 1958 film* The Seven Hills of Rome.

**Words by: Carl Sigman**     **Music by: R. Rascel**

places, City of a million warm em - brac - es Where I found the one of all the fac - es far from home.

_____ Ar - ri - ve - der - ci Ro - ma _____ It's time for us to part. _____ Save the wed - ding

Bm7  Bb maj.7

Am7  D11  G  Cm  D7

G

B7  C  E7  Am

bells    for my re - turn - ing    Keep my lov-er's arms out-stretched and

yearn - ing    Please be sure the    flame    of love keeps    burn - ing in her (his)

heart._____    Ar - ri - ve -

der - ci Ro - ma.

# Galway Bay

**Words and Music by: Dr. Arthur Colahan**

*There is no spot in Ireland as beautiful and as Irish as Galway. Though it faces the turbulent North Atlantic, its waters are gentled by the isles of Aran. Even in our modern time, its beaches are clear and clean, its meadows are emerald green and its air "perfumed by the heather." Sure, and it's a spot that has moved Irish bards to eloquence and all Irishmen to a fierce pride. Since it was written in 1926, this song has taken its place alongside "Danny Boy" and "Wearin' of the Green" as a rallying cry and, to Irishmen everywhere, as a hymn to home. In its poignant, poetic way it decries the harsh fact of British domination—ironic, since its composer, a prominent neurologist, was British!*

Freely and moderately throughout

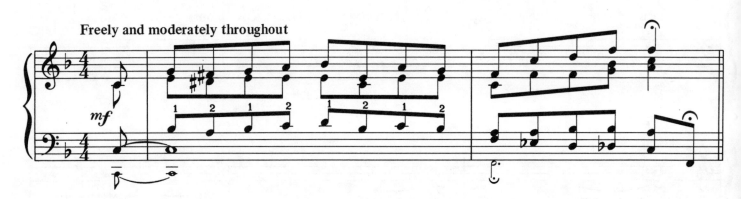

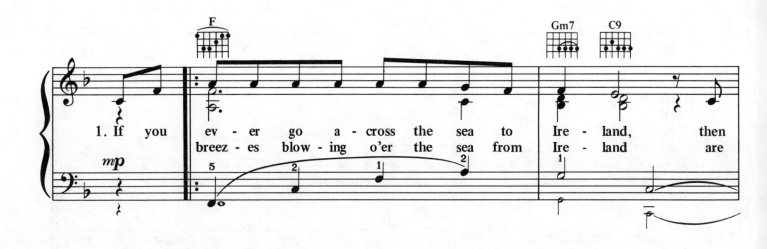

1. If you ev-er go a-cross the sea to Ire-land, then
   breez-es blow-ing o'er the sea from Ire-land are

may-be at the clos-ing of your day, you will
per-fum'd by the heath-er as they blow, and the

sit and watch the moon rise o-ver
wo-man in the up-lands dig-gin'

254

# IF

In this Jet Age, a song can become a 'round-the-world hit within a few weeks, but in 1934 tastes differed radically from country to country. In England, for example, the big hit was a dramatic ballad, "If"; in the U.S.A. the public ear was tuned to light movie love songs and swing-band rhythms. But by 1951 the mood had changed and "big" ballads became the rage. Perry Como remembered "If" and recorded it and—after 17 years—the song became an "overnight" best-seller.

**Words by: Robert Hargreaves and Stanley J. Damerell**

**Music by: Tolchard Evans**

# Anniversary Song

By: Al Jolson
and
Saul Chaplin

The eastern European melody of J. Ivanovici's "Danube Waves" had made it a perennial favorite at Jewish weddings (although few people knew its title) long before it reached the popular hit status as "Anniversary Song." The composer first published it in his native Rumania in 1880. In 1946, while filming The Jolson Story, the tune was used to recall the warm memory of a wedding waltz, and lyrics by Jolson were added to tell the story. Al Jolson's rendition was a high spot of the picture, and his recording became one of the biggest sellers in his career. In 1947, 45 years after the original composer died, his waltz led the Hit Parade for six weeks, and to this day it is the song played at anniversaries everywhere. In 1949, Jolson, acknowledging its success for him, repeated the song in the motion picture Jolson Sings Again.

love_____ though a word_____ was not said._____

_____ The world_____ was in bloom_____ there were

stars_____ in the skies,_____ Ex - cept_____

_____ for the few_____ that were there_____ in your

eyes. Dear, as I held you so close in my

arms,　　An - gels were　sing - ing　a　hymn　to　your　charms.　Two

hearts　gent - ly　beat - ing were　mur - mur - ing　low,　"My　dar - ling　I

love　you　so."　　　　　The　night　　　　seemed to

fade　　　　in - to　blos -　　　som - ing　dawn,　　　

　　　The　sun　　　shone a - new　　　but the

# Stella by Starlight

The Uninvited *was a 1944 film starring Ray Milland and Ruth Hussey—and one beautiful musical theme by Victor Young. In discussing the theme with lyricist Washington, Young identified it as "Stella by Starlight," referring to a character in the film and the photography of the sequence it accompanied. Ned stayed with Young's title but found that there was just one place in the lyric where he could make it fit.*

Words by:
**Ned Washington**

Music by:
**Victor Young**

*Note: Melody may be doubled an octave higher as far as the sign ⊕.

# Paper Doll

In 1930 Black sold "Paper Doll" to a publisher, E. B. Marks, for a $100 advance against royalties, but neglected to mention that he himself had copyrighted the song back in 1915. It collected dust in Marks's file until 1942, when the Mills Brothers recorded their hit version. Then someone discovered that the copyright was due to expire momentarily and Marks would lose the song unless he could sign up the renewal rights. But Black was dead and it was necessary to locate his heirs. A trail of alcohol fumes led to an ancient father and ex-wife. Both were persuaded to sign, but the latter demanded a bonus—one week in New York for her and a friend as guests of the publisher. The pair spent the entire week drinking bourbon in their hotel room!

By: Johnny S. Black

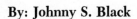

have to flirt with dol - lies that are real. When

I come home at night she will be wait - ing,___ She'll

be the tru - est doll in all this world. I'd

rath - er have a Pa - per Doll to call my own,___ than have a

fick - le - mind - ed real live girl.

# (How Much Is) That Doggie in the Window

Bob Merrill estimates that in 1952 ninety recordings were made of his songs! Victor Herbert had made it a practice to write a song a day and, compulsively, Bob felt he could do the same. But one day "inspiration ground to a halt." He tried playing free association with objects around him, scraping for an idea: lampshade, refrigerator.... Finally he spotted a stuffed dog on the bar. After a few tries he had the doggie placed in the window and the song came easily. It was introduced in a Patti Page children's album, but disc jockeys, seeing pop appeal, promoted its release as a single and it led the best-selling charts for eight weeks.

**Words and Music by: Bob Merrill**

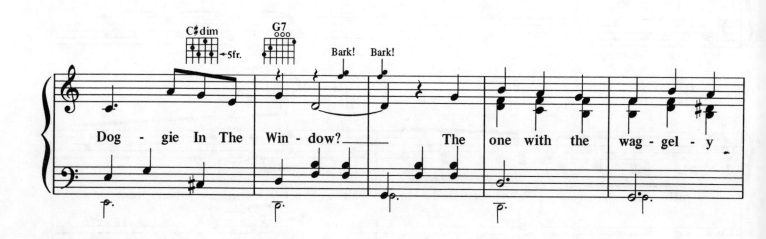

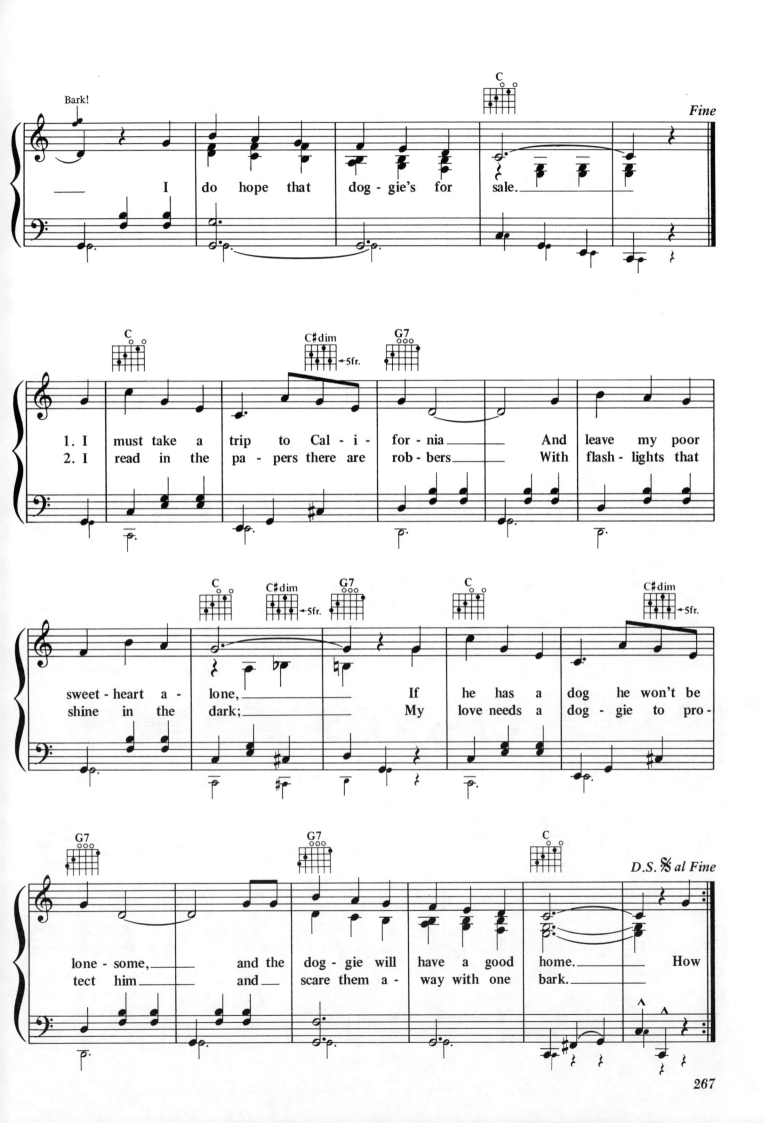

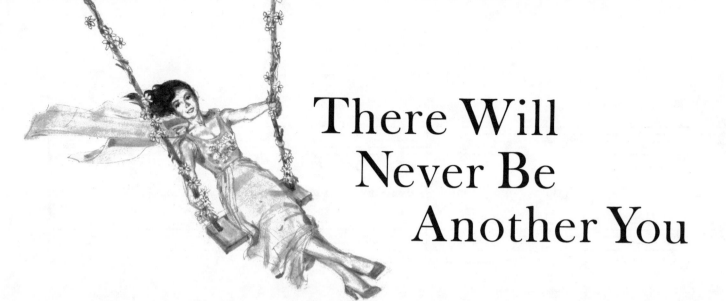

# There Will Never Be Another You

The late Sonja Henie was a better ice-skater than actress, but the Northland pixie managed to generate considerable warmth at movie box offices. Iceland, co-starring John Payne, was one of those World War II films tailored to her particular talents. Movies were more innocent then—witness this farewell scene—GIRL: "Don't forget me." BOY: "You know I won't. There will never be another you." SONG . . . The film has long since been filed away and forgotten, but Gordon and Warren's song with its fresh, long lines and provocative harmonies will always be a great favorite with musicians.

**Words by: Mack Gordon**   **Music by: Harry Warren**

# The Christmas Song

## *(Chestnuts Roasting on an Open Fire)*

*Before his birthday in 1946, Bob Wells noticed a bag of chestnuts his mother intended to use to stuff the turkey for his birthday dinner. This brought to mind New York street vendors with their roasting chestnuts, and he was inspired to write a poem, "Thoughts of Christmas." He showed it to singer Mel Tormé, who composed the tune. Christmas songs are usually recorded many months before the holiday, but the boys played "The Christmas Song" for Nat "King" Cole in early November. He was so overwhelmed by its sweet simplicity that he recorded it immediately.*

Words and Music by:

Mel Tormé and Robert Wells

spy_____ To see if rein-deer real-ly know how to fly. And

(No chord) so I'm of-fer-ing this sim-ple phrase To kids from one to nine-ty-

two. Al-tho' it's been said man-y times, man-y ways "Mer-ry

*slower*

Christ-mas to you."_____

# You'll Never Walk Alone

*Cole Porter once said that Rodgers' best songs have "a kind of holiness about them." He might have been talking about "You'll Never Walk Alone," a musical, emotional, philosophical and spiritual high point of Rodgers and Hammerstein's 1945 show* Carousel, *based on Ferenc Molnar's play* Liliom. *Rodgers' wife, Dorothy, counts this as one of her four favorite Rodgers compositions—the others are "Hello, Young Lovers," "Little Girl Blue" and a personal, sentimental favorite, "Dear, Dear," the very first love song Rodgers wrote after they were married.*

**Words by: Oscar Hammerstein II**        **Music by: Richard Rodgers**

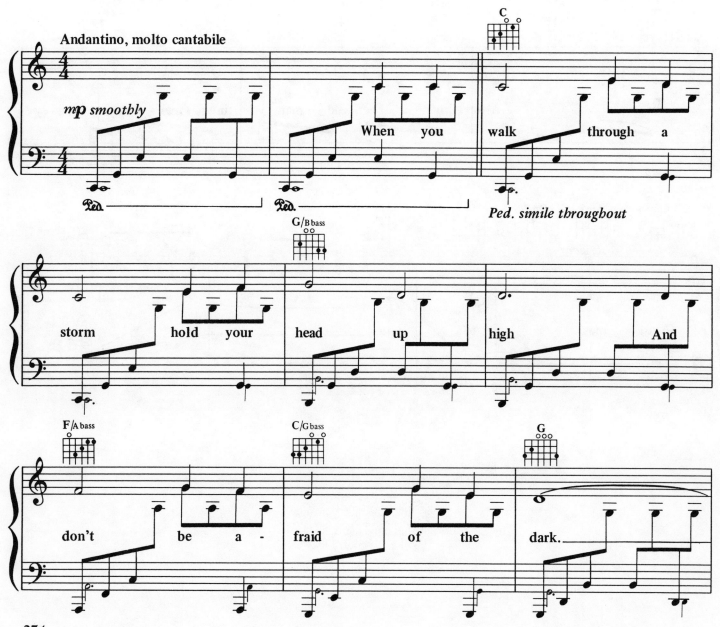

276

# May the Good Lord Bless and Keep You

One of the last lavish radio shows before TV wiped out network radio was "The Big Show," which headlined Tallulah Bankhead and presented dozens of other big stars. Willson was her music director and, as he tells it, "The broadcast took place on Sunday; so, in searching desperately for a closing-theme idea, the only thought I could get hold of was . . . my mother's weekly benediction to her Sunday-school class back in Mason City, Iowa: 'May the Good Lord Bless and Keep You.' Twenty-four hours later I taught the new song to Tallulah, who threw back her long tawny bob and broadcast the first performance from NBC's Studio 'H'. . . . Incongruous? Not for a moment—Tallu was a smash."

**Words and Music by: Meredith Willson**

G7 C G7 C
day to - day. May your trou - bles all be
F Dm7 G7 C
small ones, And your for - tune ten times ten May The
A7 Dm G7 C
Good Lord Bless And Keep You till we meet a - gain. May you
F C F
walk with sun - light shin - ing, And a blue - bird in ev - 'ry
C F C
tree, May there be a sil - ver lin - ing, Back of

# Amazing Grace

Words by:

John Newton

*Considering that John Newton (1725-1807) wrote this hymn in the 18th century, one marvels at the hold it has on today's younger generation. Teen-agers may have become aware of it first in the movie Alice's Restaurant when folk-singing hero Arlo Guthrie and friends sang the song—an old family favorite—at his hilltop wedding. Other folk singers like Judy Collins and Joan Baez picked it up and now it has gained momentum through the youthful religious revival. But whether or not one is moved by its old-fashioned message, it is a simple joy to sing and harmonize. As the song implies, Newton led a fast life in his youth, but then he was converted and became a leader of the Evangelical movement in Britain. For a time he served as a minister at Olney, where he wrote a book of hymns for his parishioners. The melody with which we are most familiar seems to have evolved in the rural South of the United States in the 19th century.*

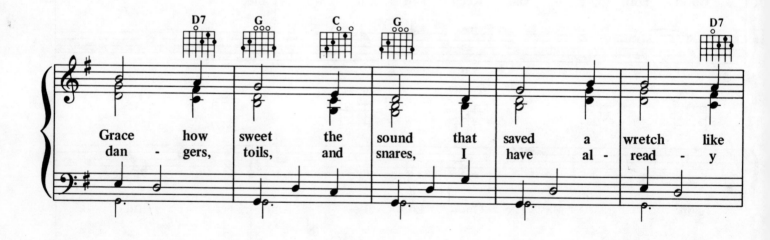

280

# (There'll Be)
# Peace in the Valley (for Me)

*In spiritual and gospel music, Thomas A. Dorsey is as big a name as the late Tommy Dorsey was in the Swing Era. Thomas A. recalls that in 1939 "while Hitler was rumbling his war chariots," he was on a train racing out of Indiana into the Ohio hills, and his eyes took in a beautiful green valley with all varieties of livestock grazing. A stream rippled down the hill, struck a rock and formed a waterfall. Dorsey took out his pencil —"If animals could have such peace in this valley, why couldn't man, with all his intelligence and ingenuity, have peace in the world." The song wasn't recorded until 1949, and then by the country singer Red Foley. It became a million-seller. About 10 years later it was a "new" hit for Elvis Presley.*

**Words and
Music by:
Thomas A. Dorsey**

# With These Hands

**Words by:**
**Benny Davis**

*One of the most moving inspirational songs of modern times originated in a wildly different concept. The title was that of a documentary film about the International Ladies' Garment Workers Union; its message: "With these hands we sew the lining in your coat," etc. But the publisher of the song envisioned a loftier theme and commissioned this song accordingly.*

**Music by:**
**Abner Silver**

*If ever it was decided to change our national anthem by popular vote, the winner —by a landslide—would be "God Bless America," a song that sums up in just a few phrases the deep love, honor and hope that we share in our great and beautiful land. When Berlin wrote his first Army show, Yip Yip Yaphank, in 1918, he cut out the song rather than risk being accused of "flagwaving." Twenty years later Kate Smith was persuaded to risk the same accusation and introduced the song on an Armistice Day radio program. Berlin, refusing to cash in on his patriotism, assigned all royalties from the song to the Boy Scouts and Girl Scouts.*

# GOD BLESS AMERICA

Words and
Music by:
Irving Berlin

# Index to Composers

Printed in the United States of America